Why God Lets People Suffer

Why God Lets People Suffer

Nancy C. Gaughan

 Magnus Press

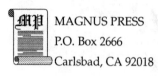 MAGNUS PRESS
P.O. Box 2666
Carlsbad, CA 92018

Why God Lets People Suffer

Copyright ©2000 Nancy C. Gaughan

All Rights Reserved. No portion of this book may be reproduced in any form without permission from the publisher.

First Edition, 2000

Printed in the United States of America

Unless otherwise noted, Scripture references are from the NEW AMERICAN STANDARD BIBLE®, Copyright ©1960, 1962, 1963, 1968, 1971, 1972, 1973, 1975, 1977, 1995 by the Lockman Foundation. Used by permission.

Copyedited by Janet Squires
LCCN: 99-80008
ISBN: 0-9654806-5-8

Publisher's Cataloguing-in-Publication
(Provided by Quality Books, Inc.)

Gaughan, Nancy C.
    Why God lets people suffer / by Nancy C. Gaughan. -- 1st ed.
      p. cm.
      LCCN: 99-80008
      ISBN: 0-9654806-5-8

      1. Suffering--Religious aspects--Christianity.
    2. Christian life. 3. Consolation   I. Title

BT732.7.G38 2000   231'.8
                                       QBI00-61

---

05 04 03 02 01 00   10 9 8 7 6 5 4 3 2 1

To

Margaret Stone Stephenson,

my first mother-in-law. Her unconditional

love, her strength in the face of disappointments

and pain, and her gift of laughter at life and at herself

taught me what it meant to live a Christian faith.

The Author's Story...

Although I spent over a year researching the Bible for this book, I did not write this book as an academic exercise. The fact is, everyone suffers. Some of us suffer more than others, but all of us will suffer sometime. My suffering began very early. Starting at age nine, I was the victim of incest for at least five years. This affected my life and left me feeling separated from other people until I was well into my 40s. This was when I learned who Jesus was and how to forgive. What glorious freedom there is in forgiveness.

My high school years were particularly hard. When a classmate shared the experiences of his parents, who were Holocaust survivors, I soon discovered that many of my father's family had been killed in camps during the Holocaust. It was during those years that, as a Jew, I learned what anti-Semitism meant. A gentile boyfriend called every night, but wouldn't ask me out because I was Jewish. My father was sentenced to prison on my sixteenth birthday (for a crime he didn't commit), and two years later my parents divorced. It was a lonely time that would have been very different if I had had someone to talk to about God. He was with me all along, but I didn't know it.

I sometimes thought I had a corner on suffering. I was not quite 21 when I nearly died in a car accident that left me with a permanent hearing loss. In my 30s my husband of 14 years left me and our two small children for a career woman. He lost a suit for custody but soon stopped paying the full child support. It was ugly and traumatic, but by then I knew God was with me. With God on my side, I was not afraid.

I next married a man who loved my children, but had a violent, unpredictable temper. He died when I was 44, leaving me with a baby barely three, a son going to college and a clinically depressed teenage daughter. During those years, God was my rock. It was shortly after that that God brought my beloved husband into my life. He led me to a Messianic rabbi who showed me that Jesus was my God too. I received Him as my Messiah and Savior, and then I was finally able to forgive myself and everyone else. I was free at last of the guilt and shame and anger of a lifetime.

Although I am happily God's servant, I still suffer as we all do. Our children and greater family do not know God, although they have accepted my love as part of my faith. I am alienated from most of my Jewish people, who insist one cannot believe in Jesus and be Jewish. We live in a town with no Messianic Jewish synagogue, i.e., a Jewish synagogue where Jesus is worshiped. The loneliness of being unable to worship with other Jewish believers at times seems overwhelming. Yet, with God at my side and in my soul, I am never alone and never without hope.

As I researched this book, I discovered how God had worked in me through the suffering He had allowed in my life. It was exciting to learn that God had been in control all along and to see that He had, indeed, caused all things to work together for good. Knowing there are reasons He lets us suffer helps us to experience joy in suffering. The joy of the Lord is my strength. This is His book.

Table of Contents

Preface 1

Chapter
1   On Suffering and God 3

Chapter
2   To Teach Us About Himself 19

Chapter
3   The Result of Freedom of Choice 33

Chapter
4   The Result of Others' Sins .45

Chapter
5   To Discipline Us 57

Chapter
6   To Show Us Our Need for Him 67

Chapter
7   To Make Us Like Jesus 79

Chapter
8   That We May Comfort Others 91

Chapter
9   To Bring Others to Faith Through God's Work 101

Chapter
10   To Bring Others to Faith Through Our Testimony .117

Chapter
11   To Contrast This Life to Eternity 131

Chapter
12   From Faith to Trust to Joy 147

Index to Bible References 155

REFACE

For years I worked with children between the ages of 4 and 12. They, like all of us, were exposed to the illness, violence, and cruelty that fill our world. Every week they talked about the suffering they saw and would ask, "Why does God let it happen?"

When I began to work with adults, I found that the adult experience of suffering is not very different from that of children, though the particulars might be different. In addition to the suffering that touched their lives and the world around them, they were burdened by guilt, anger, and fear. Like the children, they felt helpless and alone in their suffering. The question from the adults was the same as that of the children, "Why does God let it happen?" The answer is in His Word and resounds in our lives.

Recently, a woman with three children revealed the pain she had borne for eight years, when she had miscarried twins in her sixth month of pregnancy. First she asked, "Why did God take my babies?" Before I could respond, she sighed and chuckled, "I know, there are some things for which there just aren't reasons."

This book was written to let people know that there are

Why God Lets People Suffer

reasons why God allows suffering in our world. Throughout the Bible God gives us many reasons He allows suffering. In the sharing of these Scriptures, and by using real-life stories of suffering, I have three goals: (1) to show that the Bible is a trustworthy handbook for living; (2) to help people know God and to trust Him in a world filled with suffering. The source of joy that the apostles knew in the midst of suffering came from knowing God and trusting Him. By understanding His purposes in and through our suffering, we learn that God really is with us each hour, each day; (3) as we learn what the Scriptures say about suffering, we learn about God, about ourselves, and how to live as His children.

I begin every chapter with a Bible verse on which the chapter builds. But there is one verse which is the message for the whole book. I repeat it throughout, for faith in its promise will sustain us through all suffering:

> And we know that God causes all things to work together for good to those who love God, to those who are called according to *His* purpose (Rom. 8:28).

Special thanks to my mother and children who have accepted my faith as a part of me and have encouraged me to write this book. I could not have written this study without the encouragement of my friend Gloria Altemus or the support of the classes I taught and the staff of Casas Adobes Baptist Church, especially Bill Nicholson. There are no words to express the depth of appreciation and love for my beloved husband who worked with me through every chapter and revision and always reminded me that this was God's work, not mine. Finally, I thank our great God, who gave me the words.

Nancy C. Gaughan

Chapter 1

On Suffering and God

Ecclesiastes 3:1
There is an appointed time for everything

Overwhelmed by the suffering that confronted me everyday in the news, and by the suffering in my own life and in the lives of people I knew, I often prayed, "God, why do You let it happen?" It was as if He said, "I told you already. It's in my Book. That's why I gave it to you. Go read it." I did. And I found many reasons why God allows suffering in our lives.

But I also found God's loving presence in the midst of human suffering, and the certainty that He is in control of our lives. When we accept this truth and accept God's presence we can trust Him through our suffering.

Before we delve into the "whys" of suffering, we need to explore the problem of our different and changing definitions of suffering.

Our younger son and I were in the car and came to a stoplight. On the median was a bedraggled man holding a sign that read, "Homeless Disabled Vet/I am so hungry/Please help." Our hearts ached for the man. I reached into my purse for a card from the Gospel Rescue Mission. He could go there, and it wasn't all that far away. At the Gospel Rescue Mission he would get a free dinner, a shower, a change of clothes, a bed for the night and a chapel service where he would hear the gospel. The tattered man saw the card and waved it away with a laugh. "I've got a whole stack of those!" he sneered. My compassion turned to confusion and anger. Clearly he was not living the life full of blessings we were. But was he suffering? He was not homeless or hungry or dirty enough to go to the Gospel Rescue Mission. As we drove off we talked about what suffering is.

Over the course of this century we have become ever more aware and affected by the suffering of others. During the Depression, many throughout the world suffered from hunger and need. It was a collective suffering, and stories of those times are filled with talk of community, and people helping one another. World War II forced on us awareness of mankind's potential for absolute evil. Film brought suffering from across the oceans to as close as the neighborhood movie theater. With the advent of film and television, the suffering became personal as we saw the faces in the concentration camps. We began to be aware that we cannot close our eyes and hearts to the suffering of others.

Yet, the suffering was filmed from a land across the ocean. We still shut our eyes to the suffering around us. In 1950 homeless people were not allowed to loiter. We called them bums and avoided them. I don't know where they hid, or where they have come from today, but visible homeless people were few and far between in the 50s. I saw my first homeless person in a park in Chicago when I was a child. I was shocked and afraid and I asked many questions, trying to understand why that person lived that way.

Physically handicapped and retarded or psychologically ill people were also kept hidden. These children weren't allowed in our schools. They were called "disabled," not "challenged." There were no ramps in public buildings or handicapped parking spaces. How could we understand their struggles if we didn't know they even existed? We are only today beginning to see their potential as people as these children are admitted into our public schools, and celebrities like Christopher Reeve remain in the public eye.

I am thankful for the many people who view suffering as a challenge and help those who are suffering to fight back. People who view suffering that way change lives. People like those at the Gospel Rescue Mission and my mother are like that.

When I was about eight, my mother volunteered to be a Big Sister to a child whom she was told was both blind and retarded. There was no school that would take her, so she just stayed at home. Her parents crippled her with their pity, but my mother would not let this girl feel sorry for herself. She fought for the child's right to be educated and, in doing so, taught the child that life was a challenge and that she was not a loser. Instead of waiting on her, as the girl's family had done, my mother taught her to take care of herself, and, thus, taught her self-respect.

One day when reading to her, my mother noticed that she was not responding appropriately for a child who was retarded and blind. She seemed too clever to be retarded. Yet, she expressed herself in crude and babyish ways. My mother suspected that she might be deaf, but had to fight to have the girl's hearing tested. She was not retarded at all, they discovered, but deaf. She had not learned to talk properly because she was deaf—deaf and blind.

There was no question back in the 1950s of her going to a standard public school. The schools were not equipped. After over a year of fighting with authorities, my mother got her little sister into a special school. When she started school, that girl was an outcast, regarded as damaged and a thing to be pitied by her family and society. Today that little girl is a grown and educated woman, who learned from my mother not to let suffering defeat her.

In every town throughout the nation there are organizations that help the helpless. They change lives because they won't allow people to be defeated by suffering. Yet, not everyone has the gift to work with people suffering like that. As suffering seems to have overtaken our world, grief and frustration easily overcome me.

Part of the reason suffering is so much worse in our time is due to the changing definition of the word. For example, today people equate poverty with suffering. This is largely because our perception of suffering is often determined by our expectations.

My close friend's family is moving to Europe for three years. They will have to leave their beautiful house on acres of land at the foot of breathtaking mountains, their swimming pool and stone fireplace, and their modern kitchen. Her husband went on ahead to begin work and find housing. He called home distraught because there were no homes that had the comfort, convenience or beauty of theirs here. He worried about how unhappy they would be. He didn't want his family to suffer. They will suffer at least initially because they are used to the luxuries here. Yet the residents in the European town where they are moving don't see themselves as suffering because they do not know or expect other than what they have.

Although our perspectives of suffering change, most suffering is not merely relative. There are many kinds of real, not subjective, suffering. The definition of suffering I use in this book is *any unwanted pain, be it physical, spiritual, mental or emotional.* People can inflict pain on us, circumstances can inflict pain on us, and we can, and often do, inflict pain on ourselves.

Being hungry when we are on a diet or because we are fasting and praying is not suffering. Being hungry because we cannot get food is suffering. Similarly, being alone is not suffering. Feeling alone, isolated, and unloved is suffering. We inflict spiritual suffering on ourselves when we remove ourselves from God and His ways.

There is suffering throughout the world which we are helpless to end. Bad things do happen to good people, to helpless people. We are in no different times than David's when he lamented that evil flourished and the oppressed cry out (Psalm 10). No one's life is untouched by hardship or pain. With modern communications, we become aware and suffer for people we will never meet. One cannot open a newspaper or turn on a radio or television without confronting descriptions of death, disease, and cruelty. Not a week goes by without our receiving phone and mail solicitations from diverse groups, each helping a different population of suffering people. We cannot escape from the reality and the magnitude of suffering.

Our youngest was eight when he had to be taken to the doctor because of severe stomach cramping. After checking his file and examining our son, the doctor asked him, "What is *really* bothering you?"

Our son blurted out, "There are children in Guatemala who are having their homes taken away by soldiers, so they have nowhere to live. *And there is nothing we can do about it!*"

He had seen a movie in school about Central America. The doctor chided me to shield our son from the suffering in the world, but it is impossible today. Suffering is all around us.

For too many people the awareness of all this suffering leads to a path of despair. I am one of those people. I often feel helpless. Life seems hopeless. There is more hatred and violence, more hunger, illness, cruelty, and hurt than we can ever alleviate, no matter how great our efforts. For some people, God seems, at best, uncaring or even nonexistent. Many ask, "How can there be a God when such evil exists?" At worst some think He is responsible for the suffering.

Yet, God *is* here in our suffering. He tells us why He lets us suffer. The Bible is a trustworthy handbook which, among other things, shows us how to live our lives in a world of evil and suffering. Understanding God and His plan for our lives will help us have an unshakable trust in Him to bring us through any and all suffering of this world. It will also enable us to help others.

But the most important reason for this book is that in the process of learning the different reasons the Scriptures tell us why we suffer, we will also learn much more about God, about ourselves, and about what He wants of and for us.

It is not uncommon, when asked an unanswerable question for someone to exclaim, "God knows!" It is important to always remember that yes, He does. Through Solomon, He forewarned us what life would be like in Ecclesiastes 3:1-8, so we could prepare for it:

> There is an appointed time for everything,
> And there is a time for every activity under heaven.
> A time to give birth and a time to die;
> A time to plant, and a time to uproot what is planted.
> A time to kill and a time to heal.
> A time to tear down and a time to build up.
> A time to weep and a time to laugh;
> A time to mourn and a time to dance.
> A time to throw away stones and a time to gather stones;
> A time to embrace and a time to shun embracing.
> A time to search and a time to give up as lost;

A time to keep and a time to throw away.
A time to tear apart and a time to sew together;
A time to be silent and a time to speak.
A time to love and a time to hate;
A time for war and a time for peace.

These eight verses encompass all of life. We understand them through the assurance that regardless of the apparent chaos, pain, and meaninglessness in life, God is in control. There is an appointed time for everything, for every activity. God has appointed that time. He knows what has happened, is happening, and what will happen in our lives. The first step in our journey to understanding God's role in our suffering is knowing that He has allowed for it in His plan for our lives.

This list was not given to Solomon as it appears by accident. Notice that He gave us all of life's activities in pairs: A time to give birth, a time to die; a time to be silent, a time to speak. You may look at the list and say, "Of course," but as such events are happening, we rarely perceive the order because we have limited vision. We are time bound. Most people live only in immediate time. God, on the other hand, sees life with eternal eyes and knows that what we are going through now relates to our future and our walk with Him. Despite appearances, the events of our lives are not chaotic, random activities. Yet, because we can rarely see the order, it often feels like life is out of control. But if we have faith that God is in control, we are enabled to let Him work in our lives, even through the most difficult times.

There is another important lesson from these verses. There is a *time* for everything. That is, neither the good nor the bad will go on forever. There is a limit both to our suffering and our pleasure or joy. What a difference this knowledge makes!

The photo industry understands this difference. There is a seemingly endless list of the products and services related to taking pictures. We take pictures to capture the treasured moments in our lives that we all know won't last. We collect these memories and try to remember and recreate the feelings we had in those moments, knowing we cannot turn back the clock.

Why does an ice cream cone taste so good? It has its appointed time before it melts off the cone and plops on the hot sidewalk, to everyone's dismay. Those flowers in the vase are treasured all the more because we know their time of beauty is limited. Those moments are treasured, not only because they contain such happiness and beauty, but also because we know they won't last.

We need to become aware of much more than the ice cream cones of life. There are countless blessings of which we all need to become aware and to treasure, even as we treasure the flowers in a vase. Yet, most blessings go unnoticed because they are part of our everyday lives. That I can write this page means that God has given me a home, a computer, eyes, the ability to move and think, His Spirit to guide me, and a husband who encourages me. Every morning I awake with a prayer of thanksgiving for our warm, comfortable bed, for our home and health and for my beloved husband and children. These are gifts I treasure, knowing that any of them could be gone in a twinkling. They are mine by the grace of God. We all need to be aware of and thankful for God's everyday blessings.

To every extent possible, we anticipate the joys of our lives and try to plan for them. The anticipation and the planning are part of the joy, like thinking about all the different flavors of ice cream on the way to the store. What we miss is

On Suffering and God

that every moment of every day holds treasured moments, if we only become aware of them. We must hold dear the times He has appointed for us to plant, build, laugh, dance, and all the other joys God has listed in these verses. If you already do, you know the blessings most people take for granted.

We do not try to hold onto painful events. We rarely take pictures of the bad times. For emotional trials, most people try to pretend they will never happen and to forget them after they have. That is why so few people have wills. We all know that we will die, or be caught up into heaven if the Lord returns first (1 Thess. 4:17). We know there will be people who need to know what to do with the things we leave behind. We can and should plan for our deaths. Most people choose not to think about it.

Although we do not like to think about bad things happening, when we are forewarned of something, we usually prepare for it. If we knew a tornado was coming our way we all would board up windows and stockpile water and canned food in case the electricity went out. When we know winter is coming, we buy coats and gloves. Most often, people who do not look upon winter as a hardship are people who have prepared for it.

People plan and prepare for physical disasters. There is a multibillion-dollar insurance industry that attests to that. We buy insurance for when we die, when we will be sick, when our houses will be damaged or broken into, and when our cars will be damaged or stolen.

We suffer emotionally and spiritually too, but often people do not prepare because they do not realize they have been forewarned. We are generally as oblivious to the warnings of possible or impending suffering as we are of our daily blessings.

If you seek His help in trust, God will gladly turn your

personal suffering into strength and joy. *Apart from specific punishment, suffering is not caused by God, but allowed by Him.* This is an important distinction. God is good and righteous. He does not cause unjust suffering. People, however, have an incredible capacity for evil, and God often works through people. Even as He works through people to bring salvation and comfort to the world, He occasionally uses the evil that exists in man for His own purposes. The key is in understanding the part God plays in all this and why He lets us suffer. When we focus our thoughts on God, we will gain an unshakable trust in Him that will help us through any and all suffering of this life.

An unshakable trust may sound simple, but for most people those are just words. How does one trust God? What exactly are we supposed to trust? Trust requires that first we know who God is and what He has promised. Then we must trust Him to keep His word. The foundational trust is that the Bible is His word.

People have asked me, "How can anyone know God?" The answer is easy. He reveals Himself in the Bible. If one does not believe that the Bible is true, is "inspired by God" (2 Tim. 3:16), there is no way one can learn enough about God to enable him to face suffering with peace and joy. But when we study the Scriptures believing that they are true, we can begin to understand God's relationship to us. He says He is our Father and our Shepherd with unconditional, unending love. So first we must learn to trust that He loves us—each and every human being.

Then we must learn of His promises and learn to trust them. In Romans 8:28, God promises through Paul,

> And we know that God causes all things to work together for good to those who love God, to those who are

On Suffering and God

called according to *His* purpose.

There are several truths here. The first is that God "causes." That is, He has an active role in our lives. Solomon says in Proverbs that God orders our steps (Prov. 16:9). I have heard people scoff at this idea. Yet, often these same people have no explanation for an outcome that they didn't expect.

I found our baby face down in the pool, trapped by the pool cover just before his first birthday. I had no idea how to save or revive him. I had never learned CPR. In my horror, staring down at his bloated, blue, lifeless body, I wailed, "God, show me what to do! Don't let this baby die! Show me what to do!"

I had no idea what I was doing as I put my mouth over his nose and mouth and blew him up like a balloon. I don't know why I pressed on his bloated belly and chest, horrified as the pool water and vomit spewed from his little mouth. Still he was blue and lifeless. It obviously was not working, yet something compelled me to continue. At the hospital the doctors were sure there was brain damage, although they could not be sure of the extent. Today that boy is bright, athletic, and a very social ten year-old. The doctors couldn't explain his recovery, but I know it was another of God's miracles.

Two months before my twenty-first birthday, while driving home from college for the Thanksgiving holiday, I was involved in a head-on collision at a high speed on a two-lane road. According to the accident reports, the other driver came the opposite direction, pulled out into traffic, and hit my car head-on at 65 mph. It happened too fast for either of us to have seen it coming. At some point a doctor called my parents to tell them I was in critical condition and in a coma. When my father asked if the doctor thought I would survive, the doctor replied that the other woman was dying too and added that if he thought I would live, he would not have bothered to call. My head was cracked in two places. There was no expectation that I would live. That was thirty years ago. I am very much alive. Unto God be the glory. He is active in our lives.

There are numerous articles documenting stories of miracle healings and people recovering who have been the subject of prayer. The doctors who have written these articles have no other explanation than "God works." There are innumerable stories of people in war who should not be alive today. Yet they are. God works in our lives.

He works in little ways too. Not all of our needs are life threatening. My friend's husband was a new believer and skeptical of God's power in their everyday lives. When their washing machine died and their dryer broke a belt, they had only a couple of hundred dollars, nowhere near what they needed to replace them. My friend exhorted her husband to pray, but he said, "God doesn't care about this." But she prayed anyway before she looked in the paper for a used machine. Her husband was awed and humbled and praised God when He lead them to a nearly new washer and dryer for $150. When we pray for strength, patience, guidance, and compassion, He invariably provides them.

Perhaps you have heard the story of the man caught in a flood. As the water rose, a neighbor paddled by and offered to help the man escape.

"No, thanks," replied the man. "The Lord will rescue me."

As the water rose and the man took refuge on the second floor, a police boat motored by and offered to help the man evacuate.

"No, thanks," replied the man, "The Lord will rescue me."

By the time the emergency helicopter came by both the man and the water were on the roof. Again the man refused help, for, he said, he was putting his trust in the Lord.

That evening he drowned and went to heaven. He confronted God.

"I put my trust in you! Where were you?" he demanded.

"Listen, I tried to rescue you," replied God. "First I sent your neighbor, then the police, then the emergency evacuation team. Can I help it if you are too stubborn to accept help?"

It is important to recognize that God's power to cause things is beyond our comprehension, and His ways are not our ways (Is. 55:8). God often works through people. He used Moses to lead the Israelites out of Egypt, and He used the disciples to spread the gospel. He works through nature, allowing famines, disease, earthquakes, and etc. He sometimes intervenes or sends angels to intervene directly. He can and will take the lemons of your life and make lemonade, if you let Him.

God can and will cause all things to work together for good, but not for everyone. There is one condition. God does not say that He causes all things to work together for good for everyone, but only for those who love Him. Love is a choice, not just an emotion. Love is much more than feeling good and important and needed.

Love is a commitment. It is a conscious choice that translates into action. It is never selfish. Love is the willingness to put the other person's needs before your own. It is the decision, after knowing a person very well, to accept that person as the person he or she is, not for the person you want them to be. You can choose to love someone who is not trustworthy, or honorable, and who does not love you. That is what God has done. He loves us all, even those who hate Him. In sending Jesus Christ, His own son, to die for our sins, we see God's love for the whole world. We can learn how He loves us and, with the help of the Holy Spirit, seek to emulate Him and love others as He loves us.

How much easier it is to love God, who is trustworthy and loved us even before we knew Him, than to love each other. Unlike God, mankind will always disappoint us because we are human and humans aren't perfect. The more you know God, the more you will love Him. Deciding to love God means making a commitment to learn all you can about Him and to choose to believe, trust and obey Him. If we are to claim God's promise for our own, we must first choose to love Him. That is the one condition on which this promise rests.

Let's look again at Romans 8:28:

> And we know that God causes all things to work together for good to those who love God, to those who are called according to *His* purpose.

This verse does not say God causes all things to work together for good to those who love God, and also to those who are called according to His purpose, as if they were two distinct groups of people. The second phrase, "to those who are called according to *His* purpose," is connected to the first. That is, those who love God are, by definition, called according to His purpose. If you love God, He has a purpose for you. That is one of His promises to you. You can be certain God has a purpose, a plan for your life if you choose to love Him. And you can be certain of His promise that He *will* work all things to the good for you too, no matter how painful life might be at the time. Somehow, no matter what you are going through, it will work out for the good within His purpose for you.

These are promises you can hold onto. As we learn of the

reasons He lets us suffer, remember to hold on to His promises. The reasons will help you understand. The promises will sustain you.

Chapter 2

To Teach Us About Himself

Job 40:8
Will you condemn Me that you may be justified?

We would know little about God without the Bible. But if we don't know what is in the Bible or refuse to acknowledge the Bible's truthfulness, God may choose to teach us about Himself through our suffering. For example, many people who do not understand who God is are eager to blame Him when life doesn't fit their sense of justice. That was Job's error. But unlike Job, we have the Bible to teach us about God. Yet sometimes God may allow suffering in our lives to draw us closer to Him, so that we can understand Him better.

This is exactly what happened to some people in biblical history. They made mistakes we commonly make in our assumptions about God. In each case God let that person suffer in order to teach him about Himself.

My son and I often play Twenty Questions to pass the time as we drive across town on errands. He started once, and I had to guess what he was thinking when he asked questions that could be answered by "Yes" or "No."

"Is it alive?" I asked.
"Yes."
"Is it a plant?"
"No."

"Aha," I thought. Now I was getting somewhere. If it was alive and not a plant, it had to be an animal. I went through the animals. It was not a mammal, a bird, an insect, a reptile, an amphibian, or a fish. I was confused. Then again, maybe he was confused. "Are you sure it is an animal?"

"I never said it was an animal."

"Is it an animal?"

"No, and that's question number seven," chuckled my son.

I fruitlessly named a couple of one-celled creatures that are in fuzzy ground between plant and animal. I could not imagine anything that was alive and could not be classified. He insisted that it was living.

"Okay. I give up. You win. What is it?" I conceded.

"God!" he laughed triumphantly.

"Not fair." That was not a fair answer because even if we had a million questions, we couldn't put God into the same box all other things of this world fit into. We tend to think everything can be classified as animal, vegetable, or mineral, solid, liquid, or gas. Although God created all those, He is none of them.

We cannot understand God in human terms apart from Scripture because He is not merely who we think He is or would like Him to be. As one of my friends says whenever we talk about God, "We humans have such puny minds." God does not think and act the same way human beings think and act.

> "For My thoughts are not your thoughts, neither are your ways My ways," declares the Lord (Is. 55:8).

Most people throughout the world believe there is some form of higher power. They have learned of God through their own experiences as He said they would in Psalm 19.

> The heavens are telling of the glory of God;
> And their expanse is declaring the work of His hands.
> Day to day pours forth speech,
> And night to night reveals knowledge (Ps. 19:1-2).

This psalm says that our ability to know of God's existence comes through our experience of nature. The complexity and regularity of our universe shouts His name. A person needs only to experience the cycles of nature and of life to know there is a God. The number of avowed atheists are few compared to the population of the world because the regularity of the days and nights demands recognition that creation was no outcome of an accident. Even communist repression could not and cannot drive out the knowledge of God within people's hearts and minds. The more we explore space, the greater is our awareness that the universe is too perfect not to have had a creator, a superior mind and power who created all that exists and set everything in motion.

God said through Solomon, "Every man's way is right in his own eyes" (Prov. 21:2). Because human beings are the products of different experiences, cultures, and histories, each of us has a different idea about God. All of the different religions and beliefs men have held throughout the ages arose as each culture and each age has tried to define this all powerful creator in their own context.

The great diversity in man's ideas about God illustrates why we need the Bible. To know that there is some higher power requires only experiencing nature; but to know God, we cannot depend solely on our own experiences, cultural biases, and histories. Without our Bible we would be no different from any of the other religions built on faith without knowledge. The Bible is our source of knowledge. It establishes who God is and why we are here. It also tells us why He lets us suffer. We would know very little about Him were it not for His Word.

Additionally, the Bible was given to us so that we might see ourselves in the people of the Bible and learn from them who God is. Job, Jonah and Paul were three men in biblical history who thought they knew God. They relied on their own understanding, and all had erroneous ideas about God.

Job complained that his treatment wasn't fair. He demanded of God an explanation for the suffering of righteous people like himself, when the wicked seemed to go unpunished (Job 24). God answered that Job was no judge of righteousness, that compared to the holiness of God, none of us is righteous (Job 38-40). Job was not restored until he acknowledged that God was beyond his own understanding and was not answerable to Job. Through his suffering, Job came to understand the nature and character of God.

Job's demands were no different than a man I met who told me he no longer believed in God, because if there were a God, He would not allow all the suffering in the world. That man was crushed by the suffering he saw, but instead of turning to God and the Bible for answers, he turned away.

There are two ways we can refuse to acknowledge God's supremacy over our lives. Job and the man I met both blamed God for what they saw as unjust suffering and became angry with God. Another way to ignore God's love and sovereignty is by refusing to acknowledge all that He does in our lives. Recently, I talked to a man who was dismayed that he had just blown an interview for a promotion. His career had developed rapidly in his first few years as he earned his promotions easily. But for the past few years he was stuck in a position and he couldn't understand why. He had even prayed

TO TEACH US ABOUT HIMSELF

before going into this last interview in which he'd done so badly. I asked him if he had thanked God for each promotion, and he just stared in shocked embarrassment. It hadn't occurred to him that God was involved with his life.

That man is not unusual. The tendency is for us to try to make God conform to our own image of what He should be. When we don't acknowledge or trust in God's power and knowledge and righteousness, we are like the Old Testament prophet Jonah.

Our God is an awesome God, all powerful, all knowing, ever present and sovereign. Jonah knew this from the Scriptures, for he lived during the time of the prophets, eight centuries before Christ. Yet when God confronted Jonah, he reacted in the same way many of us do today.

God is a forgiving God, and He wanted Jonah to go to Nineveh to warn the people that unless they changed their evil ways, God was going to destroy them. Jonah did not want to go because he knew that the people of Nineveh were extremely evil. Like Job, Jonah wanted justice. Jonah did not want to give the people of Ninevah a warning or a second chance.

Jonah was a man no different than many of us. Forgiveness does not come naturally—anger does. Ted Bundy's story is a prime example. The state of Florida executed him in January of 1989 for luring and murdering young girls. In May of that year *Focus on the Family* aired a two-day broadcast entitled "A Look at Ted Bundy." Dr. James Dobson shared Bundy's history, his confession, and his profession of faith in Jesus Christ. Dr. Dobson discussed the genuineness of the conversion with John and Marsha Tanner, the two people who knew Bundy best. They had read the Bible and prayed with him for two years before his execution. In the broadcast of May 26, they also recounted the moral outrage of the country and celebrations of Bundy's execution. Surprisingly, the Tanners experienced threats for their role in Bundy's salvation. I understand the outrage, and yet I know that in demanding God not forgive such people as Ted Bundy, we are like Jonah in trying to limit God to our own understanding and sense of justice.

Our newspapers are filled with sin and violence. People act out the feelings of Jonah when they attack homosexuals and when they murder doctors who perform abortions. But this extreme hatred of evil people is not God's doing. God hates sin, not people. His work in our lives is to call sinners to salvation in Jesus Christ. We are commanded to forgive as God forgives us (Matt. 6:14); to love and pray for those who persecute us (Matt. 5:44); and to overcome evil with good (Rom. 12:17-21). For us to do otherwise opens ourselves to the same sin as Jonah, limiting God to our own sense of righteousness. Look what happened to Jonah.

He tried to run away from God by boarding a ship going in the opposite direction. The ship was soon pounded by a deadly storm. It became plain that they would all be destroyed at sea unless Jonah was thrown overboard. None of the men on the ship knew of Jonah's God, our God. They all thought they were throwing Jonah to his death, as did Jonah. The Lord had a large fish swallow Jonah, where He was kept safe. Jonah had to learn that, because God is all knowing, he could not hide from Him by running away as he could hide from a man. He also had to learn that God is all powerful, commanding even the sea and the fish that had swallowed him. He would learn to obey when God commanded, even if he didn't like it or didn't understand it. Once Jonah acknowledged God's sovereignty he was released safely on land.

Jonah's story shows us that we can't run away when our

limited understanding of God makes His commandments unacceptable—commandments such as forgiving and loving our enemies. Most people have heard of Jonah, yet we still try to run away.

My life serves as an example of Job, of having to suffer to learn who God is, and of Jonah, trying to run away from what I knew God wanted me to do.

As a child I was a victim of sexual abuse. For most of my life I was in bondage to the hurt I bore, having been brutalized as an innocent child. For most of my life I felt dirty, unlovable and guilty. I limited God in thinking He would not and could not cleanse me. I thought He would not forgive me and should never forgive the person who abused me from the age of 9 until I was about 14. I ran from Him and from myself by immersing myself in the world. But one day I heard that Jesus had willingly died to take all my sin upon Himself and cleanse me. As Isaiah wrote,

> Though your sins are as scarlet, they will be as white as snow; though they are red like crimson, they will be like wool (Is. 1:18).

When I accepted God's forgiveness for all sinners, I forgave both myself and my abuser. I was born anew. I had spent my life suffering under the clouds of guilt and shame because I had limited God to my understanding of His mercy and righteousness. People cannot believe that I am not bitter. Many demand, "How could God allow such a thing to happen to you? You were just a little girl!" Yet, having been raised without Jesus, through suffering I came to experience Christ. I learned who God is and how He can lift us out of despair by the power of His love.

When my first husband left me and our two young children for another woman, I was hurt and angry, very angry. When he sued for custody and then withheld child support, I was all but consumed with anger. I demanded that God punish my ex-husband. The man had sinned against God in his adultery and sinned against me and the children. Like Job, I demanded of God, "Why are the righteous being punished and the unrighteous prospering?"

But God wanted me to forgive my ex-husband and let Him handle the rest. I did not know the gospel then, and rather than confront my unforgiving heart, I ran away. I got too busy to think about it. I remarried and had a husband, a house and three children to care for. I was also neighborhood mom, a soccer mom, and a scout mom. I taught part time, was active in our synagogue on the sisterhood board and sang in the choir. Busy, busy. I was running from God, who wanted me to forgive my former husband and to rejoice that He was with me through it all. I wanted justice, not forgiveness, so I ran away in all my activities. I suffered because my anger separated me from God. We cannot feel His love when our hearts are filled with anger. I was like Jonah, and God sent storms into my life until I accepted God and what He wanted me to do.

Approximately 150 years after Jonah was there, the people of Nineveh, having known God, turned their backs on Him and returned to their vile ways. God let the city be destroyed in 612 B.C. It was all in God's time and God's plan. It worked out just as Jonah had wanted it to in the long run. The problem for Jonah was that he wanted God to act according to his script.

God has punished my ex-husband and the person who abused me. He's done it in His time and in His way. It was not for me to understand His timing or His righteousness. I have learned to trust God and to lay my hurt and anger at His

To Teach Us About Himself

feet, but I had to suffer to learn those lessons.

Job and Jonah were real people who did not understand God. If we do not see ourselves in the people of the Bible and learn from them who God is, we too may have to suffer to learn more about Him. Often, it is only through suffering and our waywardness that God can get our attention. Then He creates in us a teachable heart. That is what happened to the man who had not given God the credit for his successes, and that's what happened to Saul of Tarsus, who became the Apostle Paul.

Saul was raised a Pharisee. The Pharisees arose formally around 130 B.C. They believed that the oral interpretations of the Bible were sacred and taught that fellowship with God came not through faith, but through obeying their rabbi's interpretation of God's commandments. They focused on what people did, not on their heart attitude.

We need to try to keep God's commandments. The second commandment promises blessing to those who love God and keep His commandments (Ex. 20:6 and Deut. 5:10). Jesus said, "If you love Me, you will keep My commandments" (John 14:15). Love must come first. Obedience is an expression of our love for God.

But the Pharisees closed their minds to the sections of God's word that focused on love. To Saul, doing the commandments, regardless of one's heart attitude, was the only way to God. He believed that anyone who taught otherwise blasphemed. Jews who believed in Jesus—and there were multitudes of them (Acts 4:1-4)—taught that the only way to God was faith that Jesus was the promised Messiah (John 14:6). So Saul was enraged as Jesus' disciples went about saying that it was faith in Him, not works, that reconciled man to God.

Saul saw the devil in Jesus' words of love. Saul was sure that these men were destroying all that had held Jewish life together: performance of the Law. Like Job, Saul was angry because of his ignorance. Job thought it was unfair for the righteous to suffer when the guilty seem to go unpunished. Saul thought the way he had been taught to get to God was the only right way.

When we talk to people who don't know our God of the Bible, we must remember that sometimes it takes God's direct intervention to convince people of His truth. Our son came home from school one day wanting to talk about a classmate who told him that we were all put on earth to have fun, and he was going to have as much of it as he could. School was good only as long as it was fun. Our son knew if he tried to tell the boy that God has a purpose for each of us, his classmate would have laughed at him. How could he convince him that what the boy thought was fun would one day get him in trouble? I told him to pray for the boy because often our testimony isn't received. When our testimony isn't received, God will sometimes intervene.

Saul, for example, had to suffer in a dramatic way to learn who God is.

> Now Saul, still breathing threats and murder against the disciples of the Lord, went to the high priest, and asked for letters from him to the synagogues at Damascus, so that if he found any belonging to the Way [Those who believed in Jesus], both men and women, he might bring them bound to Jerusalem. As he was traveling, it happened that he was approaching Damascus, and suddenly a light from heaven flashed around him; and he fell to the ground and heard a voice saying to him, "Saul, Saul, why are you persecuting Me?"
> And he said, "Who are You, Lord?" And He said, "I am

Jesus whom you are persecuting, but get up and enter the city, and it will be told you what you must do."

The men who traveled with him stood speechless, hearing the voice but seeing no one. Saul got up from the ground, and though his eyes were open, he could see nothing; and leading him by the hand, they brought him into Damascus. And he was three days without sight, and neither ate nor drank (Acts 9:1-9).

God did not cause Saul to be blind and unable to eat or drink for three days to punish him for persecuting Christians. He needed to create in Saul a teachable heart. Saul, who became known as Paul in the Greek-speaking world, needed to learn that Jesus was the one of whom Saul's own Scripture had spoken. So the Lord blinded Saul and made him unable to eat or drink.

To Paul, it had to have been terrifying. He knew he had agreed to the stoning of Stephen as a follower of Jesus (Acts 7:58), and knew what he intended to do to those he had found in Damascus who believed in Jesus. Now, here before him, was Jesus, whom he knew had been crucified. In an instant Paul was confronted by the fact that what he believed was not true. Jesus is God. We can only imagine what Paul thought or felt in those three days while he was blind and unable to eat or drink.

I talk to people about God all the time. Few are as hostile as Saul was. Few even realize that they have staked their lives and their eternity on their belief that Jesus is not the Son of God and the Savior of the world. When I talk to them of God in my life, some listen, but others smile or brush me off or get angry. I want to warn them of the suffering they may have to endure to learn this same lesson of who God is. Yet, is there anything more tragic than God letting someone suffer to teach him about who He is, and the person *still* refusing to learn? What if, even after his confrontation with Christ, Paul had persisted in stubbornness?

My brother is one of those people. He was a successful lawyer and real estate developer, living on an estate with his loving wife and three beautiful, talented children. He is also a victim of Lou Gehrig's disease. Now he sits in his chair, able to move only his eyes and barely his mouth. When he could still talk, I tried to talk to him about his need for our Savior. His response was, "My God is perfect. He never gets angry and would not eternally punish anyone who has a repentant heart." When asked where he got his ideas of what God is like he replied, "Experience. My 50+ years of life." When I told him that the Bible is our only source for truth about God, he replied that everyone has his own idea of truth.

I believe that God is calling my brother through this illness in order to create in him a teachable heart, like He did with Job and Jonah and Paul. I pray and trust that God will save him, whether He heals him or not. Eternity lasts much longer than this life. I fear for all my family who refuse to learn from their own Hebrew Bible, where God reveals who He is.

I know I will never have complete knowledge about God. He is beyond total human understanding. Yet the Bible does teach us much about God—what He wants us to know. The most important lesson I have learned is that when God is beyond my understanding, He wants me to know—He wants us to know—that He is in our lives, and He will always fulfill His promise of Romans 8:28.

It is the same lesson Job, Jonah and Paul learned, the central lesson of this book: When God moves beyond our ability to understand, we must trust Him. When we condemn God because we do not understand and when we try to run away

To Teach Us About Himself

when we know what He wants us to do, we show we have not learned the lessons for which Job and Jonah and Paul had to suffer. We have the Bible to show us that God is trustworthy. We can study the Scriptures and learn from others who have studied the Scriptures, but sometimes—sometimes—God lets us suffer in order to learn who He is and how much He really loves us.

When we are suffering, we can cry out as the Psalmist did, "Give me understanding according to Your Word" (Ps. 119:169). The understanding of God and His purpose for our lives comes from God Himself as the Holy Spirit enlightens our minds, comforts our hearts, and opens up His Word.

Trust God in any kind of suffering. He will never fail you nor forsake you.

Chapter 3

The Result of Freedom of Choice

Joshua 24:15
Choose for yourselves today whom you will serve

I was in a terrible hurry to get my preschool daughter to nursery school so I could attend my class at the university. I had let her play in the sandbox in the back yard because I knew she would not wander from there. It was time to go, and she was in stocking feet.

"Where are your shoes?"

"I don't know."

"You were out here with your shoes on five minutes ago. Go find them."

"I can't. An alligator ate them."

"No it didn't. We have no alligators in Pennsylvania. Go find your shoes."

"You're right. An alligator didn't eat them. A frog did."

We eventually found the shoes behind a bush, where she had put them and forgotten. She had lost them and did not want to take the responsibility for finding them. Her childish avoidance of responsible behavior has fast become the behavior of adults in America today.

Accepting responsibility for our own choices does not come naturally for us. Yet, because we have been given freedom of choice, God holds us accountable for our choices and allows us to live with the consequences of wrong choices.

In the first chapter we looked at Romans 8:28, and one of the important lessons it contains, that "God causes," that He is in control of our lives as long as we allow Him to be; and that He, knowing how our suffering fits into His overall plan for our lives, will cause all things to work together for good for those love Him.

People ask, "What does 'God causes' mean? If God causes, how much does He cause? How much does God control and how much do people control themselves?" This is a point of great disagreement among theologians because it calls into question the extent to which God has predestined our lives.

Jeremiah wrote (Jer. 1:5) that he was appointed by God to a prophetic office even before he was born, and Paul wrote of the predestination of all believers in Romans 8:29-30 and Ephesians 1:4-5. But Jeremiah's reflections on his life and calling did not negate a God-given free will to make his own choices. And Paul's words speak only of a predestination to Christlikeness: "For those whom he foreknew, He also predestined *to become* conformed to the image of His Son . . ." (Rom. 8:29). None of these scriptures even suggest that God controls our wills and predestines everything we say and do.

Thus, it is reasonable to believe that predestination spoken of in Romans and Ephesians is based on God's foreknowledge and plan for our lives, for Scripture makes it absolutely clear that God has given us free will. Sixty-one times in the New Testament we are told, "Whoever..." Jesus does not say, in Matthew 12,

> "The person who is predestined to do the will of My Father who is in heaven, he is My brother and sister and mother."

Rather, the verse says,

The Result of Freedom of Choice

"For *whoever* (italics mine) does the will of My Father who is in heaven, he is My brother and sister and mother" (Matt. 12:50).

It is up to us to choose to do God's will rather than our own will. Our freedom of choice was established from the beginning. It is a point so simple and obvious many people overlook it.

> Then the Lord God took the man and put him into the garden of Eden to cultivate it and keep it. The Lord God commanded the man, saying, "From any tree of the garden you may eat freely; but from the tree of knowledge of good and evil you shall not eat, for in the day that you eat from it you shall surely die" (Gen. 2:15-17).

God does not want Adam to eat from that tree. If Adam eats from that tree, he will die. When things are that serious we, as parents dealing with our own children, put barriers to prevent our children from being able to do what is so dangerous. We buy plug covers for our electric sockets to make it impossible for them to stick something in that socket. We put high fences around our swimming pools and yards. We do not leave these dangerous situations to chance that our children might disobey us.

God could have put a barrier around the tree, or made it invisible, or put it where they could not get to it. He didn't. God left the choice of obedience with Adam and Eve. They could believe God and obey Him, or disobey Him and suffer the consequences. Like Adam and Eve, God has given us the freedom to choose. He also makes it clear that if we do not choose His way, we will suffer as a result of our decisions, even apart from God's discipline.

We have freedom of choice, and with that comes the responsibility for those choices. As a society, we Americans do not like to accept the responsibility for our own choices. Lawsuits abound because neither party wants to accept the blame when something goes wrong.

Here is a highly probable, but hypothetical example. Picture a sophomore from a university on spring break at some beach in Florida. The student is partying out on a boat in rough seas. He (or she) drinks too much, loses his balance and on a roll of the sea, pitches overboard. There ensues much yelling, screaming, frantic reaching and throwing things overboard, trying to save the student. Before they can reach him, he gets his leg caught in the propeller of the motor and is seriously hurt. His parents come and take him home, then call their lawyer. Someone must pay for this. Someone had to be at fault.

The liquor distributor is sued because some in the party were underage, although the person who bought the liquor was old enough. The maker of the boat is also sued because the safety lifelines that ran around the boat failed to hold the student when he was drunk and blindly stumbling in rough seas. The manufacturer of the motor is sued. The parents will say that the motor should have had an automatic shut off when something caught in it. They also sue the students who bought the liquor and the student who rented the boat. Finally, the US Coast Guard and the marina where the boat was docked are sued because they should have prohibited the students from leaving the marina and going out into rough seas. At no time will the student, his family or his lawyer look at the student's responsibility.

In this scenario everyone loses, even if the student's family loses every lawsuit, because everyone they sued had to go

THE RESULT OF FREEDOM OF CHOICE

through the cost and trauma of defending themselves.

We may be shocked that the student and his family did not accept the responsibility and penalties they bore for the student's choice of friends who took such risks, the responsibility of boating, or of drinking to a point of drunkenness. As outrageous as this picture may seem, our desire to foist onto someone else the responsibility and outcome for our own decisions and behavior is as old as creation. When God confronted Adam for eating the forbidden fruit, Adam responded,

> "The woman whom You gave *to be* with me, she gave me from the tree, and I ate" (Gen. 3:12).

Adam says that it is Eve's fault. Adam is implying that if she hadn't given it to him, he never would have eaten the fruit on his own. Also, he is blaming God for having given him the woman in the first place. Eve is no better.

> Then the Lord God said to the woman, "What is this you have done?" And the woman said, "The serpent deceived me, and I ate" (Gen. 3:13).

She too is saying that it isn't her fault because the serpent tricked her. She does not want to bear the responsibility for having listened to the snake. We, as people, haven't changed a bit. Ask any child who has just gotten in trouble what happened, and the child will find someone to blame.

In one of Flip Wilson's albums, he remembered being a child and repeatedly exclaiming, "The Devil made me do it!" In his comic strip "Family Circle," from time to time Bill Keane has a ghostly outline of a smiling character named "Not Me." This little ghost is always present when a lamp has been broken or muddy footprints are found on the carpet. As children just learning of George Washington, we used to laugh at a cartoon that depicted George's father confronting George as they stood beside a fallen cherry tree, an ax on the ground nearby. The caption showed George looking down saying, "I cannot tell a lie. The dog did it."

We can laugh at ourselves because we know we do try to avoid accepting blame. Yet, God will not allow us to blame others for our behavior any more today than He would let Adam get away with blaming Eve or let Eve get away with blaming the serpent. They were all guilty because they had chosen to do what was forbidden. God holds us accountable for our own decisions.

One of our daughters is clinically depressed. Because her body does not make enough of a chemical that is required to process information, she takes one pill each day. It is something she must do to function normally. It is her choice whether to take it or not. Three times in her life she chose to stop the medication. The consequences were devastating. She stopped going to school, stopped bathing, stopped even caring. Everyone suffered as a result of her choice. Thankfully, the effects lasted only while she was off the medicine. She is fine today.

There is really no difference between Job's cry, "It isn't fair," and our young son's complaint. Within a few weeks' time he had three special toys either broken or lost, mostly by other children. He cried, "Why did God do this to me?" Yet it was he who had chosen his friends. It was he who had not had the maturity to see that he should not let these kids play with his prized possessions; and it was he who had placed such great value on the toys that he was crushed at their loss. God could well have answered our son, as He answered Job, "Will you condemn Me that you may be justified?" Yes, God

The Result of Freedom of Choice

let those things happen, but our son learned valuable lessons, which, if he is like the rest of us, he will have to relearn many times throughout his life.

Whenever we make bad choices, we invariably get into trouble and God will let us bear those consequences. He tells us in Proverbs that He will not help us if our choices are consistently contrary to what we know He wants of us.

> "Then they will call on me, but I will not answer;
> They will seek me diligently but they will not find me,
> Because they hated knowledge
> And did not choose the fear of the Lord.
> They would not accept my counsel,
> They spurned all my reproof.
> So they shall eat of the fruit of their own way,
> And be satiated with their own devices" (Prov. 1:28-31).

A simple way of putting this is that if we choose to disobey Him, God will let us stew in our own juice. It does not say He will discipline us, although He will do that too.

Long before this proverb was written down, the writer of Judges gave us an apt demonstration of its truthfulness by sharing the story of Samson's life. In Judges 13 we learn that an angel appeared to Samson's mother and told her she would have a son who was to be a Nazirite from the womb to his death (Judg. 13:2-7).

Samson was to be set apart for God all of his life. We learn from Numbers 6:2-21 that the Nazirite vow was a vow of special holiness. The Nazirite vow separated a person from society by both his behavior and his looks while he went about living his daily life. The vow was usually for a specified period, not usually a lifetime. Paul, for example, was under a Nazirite vow while in Corinth. Acts 18:18 describes Paul stopping in Cenchrea between Corinth and Syria to have his hair cut in accordance with his vow. He could not have his hair cut in Corinth because that would have been before the period of his vow was over.

Samson knew from the time he was a boy all that was expected of him, such as not cutting his hair, not touching a dead body, and not partaking of anything made from fermented grapes. He knew that he was to live a life set apart, that he was chosen.

Yet he did not separate himself by either his actions or his thoughts. He was base, like so many of the Israelites we read about during the period of the judges. He had a weakness for women and violence, and he never became a holy person in any sense of the word.

Had Samson taken seriously his Nazirite vow, he would have been a man of peace. He never would have killed a lion nor continuously instigated murderous conflicts with the Philistines. He had two unhappy marriages to Philistine women that ended in tragedies, and he died violently along with 3000 Philistines when he pulled down supports for their temple in Gaza.

The trouble and suffering in Samson's life were of his own making in that he refused to follow God's plan for his life.

Many people think they can't relate to Samson because he was so flagrant in his disregard for what he knew God wanted of him and because he was so blind in repeating his mistakes. Yet Samson is no different from any of us who seek our own way before God's. We do not need to be murderers and poor judges of prospective mates to get ourselves into trouble. We might self-righteously shake our heads at Samson's stupidity, but we are no different. We repeatedly do things we shouldn't that cause us to suffer. We are all sometimes like Samson. Paul recognized this as he wrote to believers in

The Result of Freedom of Choice

Rome:

> For what I am doing, I do not understand; for I am not practicing what I *would* like to do, but I am doing the very thing I hate . . . For the good that I want, I do not do, but I practice the very evil that I do not want (Rom. 7:15, 19).

Since we have free will and we often freely choose wrong, what are we to do? Standing at the edge of the Promised Land, Moses instructed the Israelites how to survive there. His instructions will enable anyone to survive and receive God's blessings anywhere:

> "Now, Israel, what does the Lord your God require from you, but to fear the Lord your God, to walk in all His ways and love Him, and to serve the Lord your God with all your heart and with all your soul, and to keep the Lord's commandments and His statutes which I am commanding you today for your good" (Deut. 10:12-13).

If we love God, we will trust that whatever He instructs us to do is for our good. This is why it is natural for Jesus to say that if we love Him, we will keep His commandments (John 14:15). Obedience based on trust is a sign of love. Had Adam and Eve trusted that God's commandment was for their own good, they never would have eaten that fruit.

Let us look at what we know God wants of us. Throughout the pages of the four Gospels, Jesus gives us commandments and tells us how to live. There are too many to enumerate here, but let's look at a few and the natural consequences of breaking them.

In the Sermon on the Mount, Jesus tells us to be merciful, to be peacemakers, to forgive and love as we want to be loved and forgiven. To break these commandments, to be angry and unforgiving, will hurt the person who is angry more than the target of the anger. One way an angry, bitter person suffers is that he cannot feel God's love and peace at the same time he is angry. Peace cannot coincide with anger and bitterness. Anger and bitterness alienate people from God and from other people. No one wants to be around angry people. There are also physical consequences to prolonged or intense anger. Medical studies tell us that many illnesses are caused by the stress of sudden or prolonged anger. God tells us to forgive and be merciful for our own good.

He also says not to lust after another in our hearts. A woman asked me how to respond to her husband who said that all men look at women that way. He said that as long as he doesn't act on it no one is hurt, that it's natural and just part of the way men are. I asked her how she felt when her husband was eyeing other women. She felt violated. It made her feel that she was not enough for her husband, even though he had never physically been unfaithful. It *was* hurting their marriage. The more he looked, the more distant she grew. The commandments are there for our own good.

Jesus also tells us not to worry, but I admit that I am often disobedient. Whenever I neglect to call upon God, to turn what worries me over to Him, I get knots in my stomach. I cannot sleep well. I become irritable and short tempered with those around me, and can do nothing well because my mind is focused on the cause of my anxiety. I have a choice. If I choose to, I can pray for God to take the burden from me, to take over the situation. I can then trust God to take care of the situation that causes me such worry. He has never failed me. He will see us all through our crises. When I don't choose to trust Him and I worry everyone around me suffers.

Our most important choice is choosing to believe that the

The Result of Freedom of Choice

Bible is true and that Jesus is who He said He is. Without our choosing to believe in Jesus' sacrificial, atoning death on the cross and subsequent resurrection, the natural consequence of that choice is eternity away from God. Jesus, God's Son, is His way to fellowship with our Heavenly Father.

As we become aware of what God wants of us, we are to use what we have learned and obey His commandments. When we choose to follow our own plan, rather than God's, we should not blame God for the suffering that is the result of our own choices. God has nothing to do with it.

But choosing to follow Christ and commit our lives to God's ways results in a life of peace and joy now and for eternity.

Chapter 4

The Result of Others' Sin

Joshua 22:20
And [he] did not perish alone in his iniquity

When we sin, others are hurt. The greater our sphere of influence, the greater will be the magnitude of other people's suffering. Both the Bible and our lives affirm this. Because this is true, we have grave responsibilities in our own behavior.

The Bible is a very exciting book to me because it is literally the Book of Life. By that I mean that it is more than an instruction book of how to live this life and how to obtain everlasting life, although both of those aspects are part of the Bible's excitement. It is also exciting for me to see how life *today* is described in its pages. Our lives continually verify the truth of the Scriptures. It is this changeless and timeless nature of the Bible—the nature of God Himself—which certifies it as an instruction book we can depend on. We can live life as we want, mess up our lives and try repeatedly to pick up the pieces, or we can read and learn from the Bible and save ourselves endless grief. For example, the Bible tells us plainly that when people sin, others suffer. If you thought about it, you would know that from your own experience as well.

All too often, sometimes with tragic results, those who sin overlook the suffering they cause in other people's lives. There are two reasons the connection is often missed. First, the people who suffer in this way are not always immediate players in the sin. Often they are numberless and anonymous to the person sinning. Second, the suffering that comes as the result of others' sins often occurs over a long period of time.

For example, the commandment "Do not steal" is very simple. There are no qualifiers. It does not go on to say that it is okay to steal if no one is looking or if you don't get discovered. It does not say it is okay to steal if you don't know from whom you are stealing, like stealing from the government. Nor does it say it is okay to steal from people or organizations that you think don't deserve so much money. It doesn't even say that the only thing we shouldn't steal is money. It just says don't steal—anything—under any circumstances, ever. It is very simple. When people violate it, not only is the target of the theft hurt, but others are also.

I noticed a new sign on the door as I entered a grocery store. The sign asked people to check all their packages and bags with Customer Service when they entered. There are few stores that don't have surveillance cameras and mirrors. I know the stores must do these things to protect themselves, but they make me feel violated. I don't like going where people feel they must protect themselves from me. They don't trust me, and it isn't my fault. I have done nothing wrong. I have stolen nothing since I took a box of crayons at the grocery store when I was about five years old and my mother made me take it back and apologize. We are all suffering the stores' mistrust because others have sinned. The shoplifters have broken trust with the stores so they can no longer trust any shoppers.

If a home in our development is broken into, everyone in the development feels vulnerable. If a person is mugged in a shopping center parking lot, everyone who shops there is threatened. Each theft is a sin against God, yes, but also against all of society.

The psychological damage is only a part of the suffering we endure because of the sin of stealing. Shoplifting raises the prices the stores must charge everyone. Medicare fraud, tax evasion, welfare fraud, and all governmental fraud raises our taxes to make up the deficit. Burglary and robbery of anyone raises everyone's insurance premiums.

Some steal from insurance companies by filing false claims. Insurance fraud does much more harm than just raising our insurance premiums. It also raises all our medical costs as liability insurance goes up for doctors, pharmaceutical companies, and hospitals. False insurance claims also raise costs on products as their liability rates go up. So when a person steals from anyone, he steals from everyone.

That is just one commandment, and everyone knows stealing is wrong. In our society today, adultery is not even considered a crime because it is said to be "victimless." Yet, just as "Do not steal" is simple and straightforward, so is "Do not commit adultery." No excuses.

No matter how bad our marriage is, we may not commit adultery, not even in our minds. If wayward husbands and wives put half the energy into salvaging their marriages that they put into trying to get someone into bed, their marriages might have been all they needed. I had first hand experience when I was a single mom. Married men talked to me of adultery as harmless, even good. We were two consenting adults, they argued. The usual, but far from only, scenario was that he was not happy at home. His wife was his friend, but not his sweetheart or his lover. He reasoned that if he could satisfy that need for physical excitement elsewhere, no one would know, and he would be happier at home. No one would be hurt—or so they argued.

Our son was nine and our daughter was six when their

dad left me for a career woman in a distant city. He told our children that he was leaving me, not them. All they knew was that their family would never be the same again. Our son sobbed when he learned his father was moving down to sleep in the family room, not in our bedroom. When he was twelve, our son swore he would never marry, that he would never risk putting his children through what he and his sister had endured. Now he and his sister are in their 20s. Both are living with a significant other. Neither is in a hurry to marry. Don't try to tell them that adultery only affects the consenting adults. Sadly, neither child sees that what they are doing is also sin and that their families are suffering as a result.

God commanded us not to commit adultery because He knew what adultery does to families. Can a husband or wife who lies about where they've been and who they've been with be the same person who has no need to lie? It *has* to hurt the family. What child won't be hurt by parents who lie, parents who put their own desires above the child's need? As Doc the barber told my son, "The nicest thing you can ever do for your children is to love their mother." One cannot love one's spouse and commit adultery.

Our lives are mirrors of the stories of biblical people. The Bible repeatedly shows us that when someone sins, others will suffer.

Achan was just another soldier in the Israelite army when they prepared to take Jericho. Just as the priests were blowing their rams' horns and the guards with the ark finished circling Jericho for the seventh time, Joshua instructed the people that everything in Jericho belonged to the Lord. No one was to keep anything for themselves.

> "But as for you, only keep yourselves from the things under the ban, so that you do not covet *them* and take

THE RESULT OF OTHERS' SIN

some of the things under the ban, and make the camp of Israel accursed and bring trouble on it. But all the silver and gold and articles of bronze and iron are holy to the Lord; they shall go into the treasury of the Lord" (Josh. 6:18-19).

Through Joshua, God told the people in language as simple as "Do not steal," that when they entered Jericho no one should take anything. They were told to take nothing lest they "make the camp of Israel accursed and bring trouble on it." Our Father does not make idle threats. He tells us what we may and may not do and the consequences of our choice of behavior. He warned the Israelites not to take anything, lest a curse be over the whole nation.

We learn from Joshua 7 that that was exactly what happened. One man, Achan, took and hid "a beautiful mantle, two hundred shekels of silver and a bar of gold fifty shekels in weight" (Josh. 7:21). Then the Israelites tried to attack a small town of Amorites, Ai. The spies sent by Joshua recommended only 3,000 Israelites go and fight because it was such a small town. But the Israelites were routed and forced to retreat when thirty-six soldiers were killed at the outset. Those men were innocent of having violated the ban. They died because Achan had sinned.

When the Israelites were beaten, Joshua understood that God had removed His shield from around them. Joshua and the elders of the Israelites tore their clothes, put dust on their heads, as men in mourning, and fell on their faces before the ark, crying out to the Lord (Josh. 7:6-9).

God reminded them that He had warned them not to take anything under the ban. God told them to find and destroy the person who stole from Him and destroy all his belongings. When Joshua confronted Achan he confessed, and

Achan and all his family—who knew of his covetousness and thievery—were stoned, then burned completely, just as the Lord had commanded (Josh 7:19-26).

God's punishment may seem very harsh, but God called Israel to be a covenant people, and that required their obedience. If the Israelites, individually, would not be obedient, the nation as a whole would soon be infected like a plague and cursed. God made that very plain before they entered the Promised Land.

> "But it shall come about, if you do not obey the Lord your God, to observe to do all His commandments and His statutes with which I charge you today, that all these curses shall come upon you and overtake you" (Deut. 28:15).

It was important for the Israelites to see that God was as faithful in keeping His admonitions as He was in keeping His promises of blessings. He wanted their obedience to come from their love and trust in Him, but their obedience was necessary even if it stemmed from fear. And as a righteous God, He has to punish disobedience.

Children get upset with their teachers when they keep the whole table in for recess because of the bad behavior of just a few students. The goal is to teach the children that the bad behavior of a few will hurt everyone. Hopefully this knowledge will keep children in line who wouldn't care if it was just themselves who would be punished. Of course, for those children who are not taught to worry about how other people will be hurt by their misbehavior, their peers, who get punished unfairly, will pressure them into obedience in the future.

Had Achan believed that God would keep His word, he would not have taken those things any more than children

The Result of Others' Sin

will misbehave in my son's classroom once they know their teacher will punish the whole table for the behavior of one or two of them. But Achan did not believe God. Like Jonah, Achan did not understand that God is all knowing and everywhere at once. We can see that Achan's attempt to hide the booty was as foolish as Jonah trying to escape God by getting on a boat. Further, Achan did not understand that our Father is faithful to keep his promises, even those of discipline. Achan did not believe all the Israelites would be cursed for his transgression. Yet that is exactly what God promised and exactly what happened.

It is important that we understand our responsibility for the suffering of others when we sin. When we are tempted, it can keep us from sinning. Achan was an example of the suffering an ordinary man can bring on his people. The next two examples are of people with our public trust violating commandments, one of adultery and lying, the other of lying. Elected and appointed officials are responsible for the people they represent or govern. When a public person sins, the suffering is magnified.

Much has been written about President Clinton's adulterous affair with a White House intern less than half his age and about his subsequent lying under oath. He, no doubt, thought at the time that he and Monica Lewinsky were both consenting and that no one would be hurt. Now his wife and daughter, and the American people bear his shame. Whether they know it or not, the American people have been hurt by President Clinton's sin. I say, "whether they know it or not," because President Clinton's ratings have not reflected an outraged citizenry. That in itself shows one way the American people were hurt. Most of the Americans polled were willing to overlook Clinton's sins because the American economy is strong. The lack of moral outrage shows either that those polled no longer accept God's laws, or they do not believe our leaders must lead honorable lives. When Clinton cheated on his wife and lied under oath, he did more than that. He stole our respect and our faith and tarnished the image of the American people throughout the world.

Our president is symbolic of all Americans in the world's eyes. We elect our president to represent us. If it's okay for the President to commit adultery and lie under oath, it's okay for anyone in America to do the same. No longer can the people of the world accept the word of an American.

People used to respect the office of the presidency. Clinton's behavior not only gives permission to the American citizenry to behave each in his own way with no moral compass, it makes a mockery of those who trust our representatives in government to be people Americans can look up to.

We have suffered loss of faith and loss of moral standards, but that is just the tip of the iceberg. Declining morality eventually causes the decline of a civilization. One need only look at history, at the rise and fall of the nations of the Bible, of Rome, of the Soviet Union to look at the effect of moral decay on the longevity of a country. God's discipline may yet fall on the American people.

One need not be the president of a country to be a public official whose sin hurts a greater number of people. I was only fifteen years old when the mayor of our town and several city officials, including the mayor's brother, were indicted on charges of evading income taxes. In addition, they and their accountant were accused of conspiring to evade income taxes. Conspiracy is the act of planning or plotting by two or more people to do something illegal.

My father was the accountant.

As the trial dragged on, the mayor's brother couldn't stand the stress of going to court and having his name and picture in the paper every day. One day he met his brother at the door with a gun and raved that either the mayor would promise to get all his brother's charges dropped or the brother would shoot him. So the mayor, without even letting the engineer or my father know, began his plea bargaining. The district attorney was willing to drop all the charges against the brother if the mayor would plead guilty to conspiracy.

All of the charges were false. The mayor had to be willing to lie and say he had plotted with others to try to evade income taxes in order to stop the trial and drop the charges against his brother. I don't know what else he could have done, perhaps take the whole story to the newspaper and expose what he'd been asked to do. As it was, the story the papers got was from the district attorney's office, "Mayor pleads guilty to conspiring to evade taxes!"

By definition, one cannot conspire alone. My father was sentenced to three years in a federal penitentiary on my sixteenth birthday. His innocence was confirmed when the CPA review board reviewed his case, ruled him innocent, and reinstated his license.

The mayor lied to save his brother and save his life. Many people were hurt by his lie. My father and the city engineer both went to prison. Think about what that did to our families. You find out who your friends are when your parent or your spouse goes to prison. And what of all those people who had put their trust in the mayor, the engineer and my father? The mayor's declaration that he had tried to evade taxes was one more blow to public trust in elected officials. Our whole society is hurt every time someone sins in whom the public puts its trust.

These are two examples from our lives. In the Scriptures, David's life shows us the added responsibility of leadership.

David's reign certainly had its ups and downs. As a boy,

when David was good, he lived for God and the Lord raised him up from shepherd boy to an unlikely kingship. But when he was bad, he was horrid, and he paid for his disobedience. So did other people. His first sins were adultery with Bathsheba, and the murder of her husband, Uriah the Hittite. David's family was literally torn apart by his ungodly actions. The baby he and Bathsheba had conceived died. Not long after these events David's son Amnon raped his daughter Tamar, and another son Absalom led a revolt that drove David out of Jerusalem. Absalom, a son David loved very much, was killed in the fighting (2 Sam. 11-18).

There are two lessons for us in these stories. First, as individuals, knowing that our sin will hurt others, some of whom we may not even know, must strengthen us in our resolve to keep from sinning. For those who are parents, teachers, managers, coaches, group leaders of any sort, we must remember that the suffering we cause by sinning will be magnified by our positions. Whenever Christian leaders sin, inevitably some people are lead away from God because of their actions. Jesus said,

> "But woe to you, scribes and Pharisees, hypocrites, because you shut off the kingdom of heaven from people; for you do not enter in yourselves, nor do you allow those who are entering to go in" (Matt. 23:13).

"Woe to you." What a powerful warning it is. These words of warnings are for all of us in leadership positions: parents, teachers, managers, coaches, clergy—all of us.

There is a second lesson for those who suffer as a result of others' sins. We look at those who died as a result of Achan's sin and, perhaps, think how unfair it was for them. Or we think of those who suffered because of David's sins and think

The Result of Others' Sin

God had abandoned those people. Yet God never abandons those who love Him. Ultimately, this life is brief and we will spend eternity with Him.

Furthermore, there often is more than one reason for each experience of suffering. God might use the suffering that you did not create or deserve to teach you of His character or to get you to conform to the image of His Son, or perhaps for some other reason that the other chapters of this book cover.

Time and again this lesson we learn from the Bible we also learn from experience, that no matter what God may allow us to suffer, He is always there to help us through it. Throughout the pages of this book, you will read much of the suffering of my life: the incest, my father in prison, my parents divorcing, my near fatal car accident, my first husband leaving me for another woman, my second husband dying, leaving me with a college bound son, and a clinically depressed daughter and three year-old. Yet, each time I was hurt, God was there and used my suffering to work all things to the good for me. And I know that while I suffered, He suffered too. The godly King David, in his early days of suffering, wrote,

> You have taken account of my wanderings;
> Put my tears in your bottle;
> Are *they* not in your book? (Ps. 56:8).

If you are a victim of someone else's sin, turn to God. Trust Him. Let Him work to turn your suffering into good. Remember, no situation in this life is hopeless, because our hope is in our eternal life with God, bought by the blood of His Son.

Chapter 5

To Discipline Us

Proverbs 3:12
The Lord disciplines those He loves (NIV)

Discipline is a complex thing. If not done right, it breeds resentment, not correction. God is our perfect parent and He loves us. That is why He disciplines us when we go astray.

One of my family's favorite movies is *Willie Wonka and the Chocolate Factory*, starring Gene Wilder. It is the story of a candy manufacturer who wants to find a child with a pure heart to run his factory after he retires. Through a random process, he reduces the children of the world to five, four of whom are none of our idea of a dream child. As the children and their parents tour the factory, one by one their lack of discipline gets them in trouble and the child and his/her parent are eliminated from the competition.

As each are expelled, creatures called Oompah Loompahs appear and chant a little riddle that teaches a lesson about the undesirable behavior. First a gluttonous boy is sucked into a chocolate river, and they chant about gluttony and greed. When the constantly gum-chewing little girl stuffs something in her mouth that makes her expand and turn blue, they chant about obsessive behavior. The most obnoxious of the children is Veruka Salt. Time and again she sees something that is impossible and even wrong for her to have, and she explodes,

"I want it NOW!" Time and again her father is driven into a pathetic frenzy, trying to appease, rather than discipline her. When she finally grabs at a golden egg and falls down a tube for bad eggs, the Oompah Loompahs chant that when a kid is a brat, it is not the children, but the parents who are to blame.

Although there are many different theories on disciplining, I know of no books on child rearing that tell parents not to discipline at all. When a child has a temper tantrum in a store and the parents give in and buy something to quiet the child, it bothers us greatly because the child has gotten away with unruly behavior. We have that reaction because we know that by refusing to discipline the child, those parents are preventing the child from learning obedience and patience. And they are failing to teach a child how to distinguish between needs and wants. The child who does not learn that none of us gets all we want when we want it will have a life of frustration and bitterness. Or, as one of our daughters put it when she was only eight, "Why is it all the nice kids have mean moms and all the kids with moms who never yell are so mean and bratty?" She discovered by the time she was eight that discipline is an act of love.

> . . . do not despise the Lord's discipline,
> and do not resent his rebuke,
> because the Lord disciplines those he loves,
> as a father the son he delights in (Prov. 3:11-12, NIV).

None of our parents were perfect. I could write of the weaknesses and sins of my own parents, but I know that I am not a perfect parent either. Some of us have horrible examples of parents in our own lives. Still, we all have a perfect role model, our Father in heaven.

We have already explored how God handled the tree of

knowledge and Adam and Eve. God told Adam and Eve they could eat from any tree but one and told them the consequences of disobeying Him. They disobeyed Him anyway, and suffered because of God's punishment. He has also told us through His commandments what we are to do—to love Him and love each other. He also told us that we would be disciplined if we reject Him and pursue our own ways.

Perhaps the greatest gift we receive from our Father is the gift of trust. Trust is foundational to all healthy relationships. We cannot truly love someone we cannot trust. Obedience not based on trust and love will stem from fear, breed resentment and, ultimately, cause neurosis or rebellion. God has taught us that we can trust Him even when He disciplines us.

First of all, we need to trust God that He understands us and our limitations, and that if what He is asking seems too hard, He will help us. We must learn to trust that His love is forever and that He keeps His word. It is easy to obey God in love when we know He loves us unconditionally, and because of His love we can trust Him unconditionally.

At about noon one day at a warehouse store parking lot, I was in my car waiting for a parking space at the head of a row. The lot was very crowded. It was hot, and I had been waiting for a while when I spotted two women pushing a cart up my aisle. In the cart was a little boy about two years old. From the discussion, which was inescapable from my convertible, it was plain that they were child, mother and grandmother and that the child had not behaved well in the store. The boy sat, pouting in the cart, while his mother and grandmother fussed about how late they were, how hot it was, and how badly the two year-old had behaved because he had missed his nap and was hungry.

When they got to the back of their car and unloaded their purchases, they told the boy to stand up so they could more easily pick him up. He refused and they began to yell and swear at him. The angrier they grew, the more he cowered, alternately whimpering and stubbornly pouting. Finally, the grandmother got into the driver's seat and shouted to her daughter to get into the car and just leave the boy in the cart in the parking lot. That was all he could take. He let out a terrified howl. The mother repeated the threat and laughed at his terror. With the little boy wailing and clutching for her, she pushed the cart with the baby out of the way of their car and started to get into the passenger side. The little boy was beside himself, standing, screaming for his mother, who told him it was too late, that he should have stood up before. The grandmother backed up just enough for the mother to get out, snatch the child, and throw him into the back seat.

I was heartsick. I called out to the mother, pleading with her to never again so threaten and frighten her son like that. She promptly told me, amidst much profanity, to mind my own business.

I witnessed a living nightmare. If we examine what that child learned from that nightmarish scene, we can see the contrasts and establish the trust that makes obeying God such a joy. God is our Father and is everything those women were not.

That poor child learned he could not trust his mother or grandmother, because neither understood his limitations. This child was barely two years old. The women knew he had missed both his lunch and his nap. Yet they demanded he have a standard of behavior even they could not maintain. That was the first thing that made their discipline unacceptable.

We can trust God because we know our Father knows us, our limitations and our abilities. Both King David and Paul teach us that God knows us, perhaps even better than we know ourselves. Paul wrote, "For all have sinned and fall

TO DISCIPLINE US

short of the glory of God" (Rom. 3:23). David wrote, "He knows how we are made. He remembers we are dust" (Ps. 103:14). Our Father does not ask more than we can do without his help. He disciplines in love because he knows what we are capable of doing with His grace and power as our help.

A second aspect of discipline is knowing that our Father has told us what He wants us to do. One reason Jesus came to earth was to help us understand what our Father wants from us. When asked by the lawyer what was the great commandment in the Law, Jesus said,

> "'You shall love the Lord Your God with all your heart, and all your soul, and all your mind.' This is the great and foremost commandment. The second is like it, 'You shall love your neighbor as yourself.' On these two commandments depend the whole Law and the Prophets" (Matt. 22:37-40).

Of the 613 commandments that embody the Mosaic Law, Jesus says these two are essential to a godly existence. If we obey them, the others will follow. Paul explained it further when he wrote to the Romans that the outward signs, what we do, will flow freely as a natural outcome of loving God and loving our neighbor:

> The commandments, "You shall not commit adultery, You shall not kill, You shall not steal, You shall not covet," and any other commandment, are summed up in this sentence, "You shall love your neighbor as yourself." Love does no wrong to a neighbor; therefore love is the fulfilling of the law (Rom. 13:9-10, RSV).

Why God Lets People Suffer

So Jesus said in effect that what God wants us to do is love Him and love our neighbors. If we do, we will fulfill God's will for our lives.

I am not always very good at letting our son know what is expected of him. I assume our ten-year-old son knows all the rules. They do not seem to be beyond his abilities. And, after all, he's been told numerous times. Yet, often when he fails to stop playing with his food and eat, or forgets to take his toys from the family room at bedtime, or some other minor infraction, instead of reminding him of the rules, I give him "The Look." If he doesn't get the message from "The Look," I look harder, becoming angry that he is oblivious to my look and his impending doom. Eventually, I blow up, much to his surprise. And it isn't fair of me or good discipline.

This is not the role model God gives us. God tells us what He wants of us and tells us endless times. We are told 61 times in the Old and New Testaments to love the Lord, love God and love Jesus (NIV). We are told 62 times to love our neighbor, foreigners and each other (NIV). It's a simple message, Love. God repeats it over and over because we are children. Our son also needs to be reminded what he is supposed to do.

That poor baby in the parking lot also learned that when he couldn't control himself, when the task seemed too great, he couldn't trust his grandmother or mother to help him through the ordeal. He was tired and hungry. He needed them to be calm and to pick him up when he was too tired to stand himself.

We can trust our Father. We know that when life seems too much for us, God will help us through. He is a just and loving God who does not discipline without first providing for our weaknesses. God has always known, since before

To Discipline Us

Adam and Eve first ate that fruit, that mankind would never measure up to His standard.

When He brought the Israelites out of Egypt to call them His people, He established His Law. The first nine chapters of Leviticus and all of chapter 16 are about sacrifices, burnt offerings, sin offerings, and guilt offerings. The system of sacrifices embodied in these offerings were to allow the Israelites an escape from their sins and point to the day of one last, perfect sacrifice. He gave the world His Son to take away the sins, even as the bulls and goats were to take away the Israelites' sins in the Old Testament. Finally, He sent the Holy Spirit to be our Helper, Counselor and Guide. When we are burdened or tempted, suffering or sore, our God is faithful to help us. Paul, writing to the believers in Corinth, assures them and us that God will help us.

> No temptation has overtaken you but such as is common to man; and God is faithful, who will not allow you to be tempted beyond what you are able, but with the temptation will provide the way of escape also, so that you will be able to endure it (1 Cor. 10:13).

We have confidence that God has told us what He wants of us, and that He knows our limits and can and will help us. We can trust God because He has shown us He will help us when we sin.

When the mother and grandmother threatened to drive away and abandon the boy, he became hysterical. They had planted in him forever the fear that if he were bad enough, they would abandon him.

This opens another aspect of God's discipline. There are those who say we can lose our salvation. They say God's love is dependent on our behavior. This is the same position with which those women threatened the baby. The people who believe this point to John 14:15, 23-24 and John 15:10, where Scripture says that if we love Jesus, we will keep His commandments and that those who do not keep His commandments do not love Him. They further point to James' epistle, whose central theme is on the effect of faith in a person's life. James, chapter 2, in particular, emphasizes that without works faith is useless. It is dead.

But these passages do not mean that God's love is dependent on our keeping His commandments. The unconditionality of God's love is apparent throughout both the Old and New Testaments. From the time God brought the Israelites out of Egypt through the birth, crucifixion, and resurrection of Jesus, the Bible is the story of God's people as they alternately worshiped God and turned away from Him. The Bible is the story of God's faithfulness and love, despite the behavior of the Israelites. The book of Hosea is an allegory in which God has Hosea marry a harlot to illustrate God's love for His people, who time and again were unfaithful. In Psalm 136, the refrain says of God, "His love endures forever" (NIV). It is repeated in every verse.

We are told many times in the New Testament as well that our salvation is not dependent upon our works. All of us who believe are God's chosen people and He will never abandon us. Before He was crucified, Jesus told the disciples,

> "And I will ask the Father and He will give you another Helper, that He may be with you forever" (John 14: 16).

It is through our Helper—the Holy Spirit—that God's unconditional and steadfast love disciplines, shapes, empowers, and conforms our lives to Jesus Christ.

TO DISCIPLINE US

The Holy Spirit, as our Helper, bestows gifts, and is, in fact, Himself a gift, God permanently abiding in us. He is our rudder. He teaches us, reminds us, convicts us of our sins and leads us to righteousness (John 16: 7-8). And, as Jesus said in John 14:16, He abides with us *forever*. Jesus does not say, "Until you ignore His prompting and sin." It is in those times of weakness that He convicts us, not abandons us. God's love is not dependent upon our works or on whether we stumble and fall.

God our Father's love is forever. He will not abandon us. He disciplines us in love, and sustains us for Himself. It is hard to hate the sin and love the sinner, but this is what God does for us.

Finally, the little boy learned that he could not trust his mother to keep her word. She threatened to hit him, and she didn't. She told him she would leave him, and she didn't. Throughout the Bible we learn to trust our Father because He does keep His word, not only the promises, prophecies and blessings, but the discipline as well.

After King David died, Solomon became king. When God established His covenant with Solomon, He warned him,

> "If you turn away and forsake My statutes and My commandments which I have set before you, and go and serve other gods and worship them, then I will uproot you from My land which I have given you, and this house which I have consecrated for My name I will cast out of My sight and I will make it a proverb and a byword among all peoples" (2 Chr. 7:19-20).

He does not say here or anywhere else that He will stop loving the Israelites. He says that He will discipline them. We know from later commentary in the Bible that Solomon caused the Israelites to turn to other gods by his example, and that God first divided the kingdom, then scattered the Israelites to Assyria and the Judeans to Babylonia. Solomon's great temple lay in ruins for seventy years. God *did* discipline His people. Never again have Jews been idol worshipers.

For those of us who try to do good and sometimes fail, God is merciful. He has told us He loves us, and that He will discipline us so we will turn our hearts back to Him. Jesus said to the church at Laodicea,

> "Those whom I love, I reprove and discipline; therefore be zealous and repent" (Rev. 3:19).

If we mourn for our shortcomings and are repentant, trying to do better, we will be disciplined when we sin, but we will not be consumed.

A woman beset by troubles confessed to me that she was burdened and afraid. She thought God was punishing her, but she worried that she didn't know what she had done wrong. She was afraid things wouldn't get better until she confessed a sin unknown to her. I reminded her that we are children of a righteous, loving Father. The Holy Spirit will convict us of sin. That is one of His functions (John 16:8). If we are suffering because of God's discipline, He will reveal to us how we have sinned. *Sometimes we already know.*

Yet discipline is only one of the reasons God lets us suffer. If the Holy Spirit does not reveal our sin, chances are we are suffering for one or a combination of other reasons.

Because He loves us, He must discipline us. God's righteousness demands that He punishes sin, and it is through His discipline that we learn. It is as if He says, "I love you too much to let you get away with that."

Chapter 6

To Show Us Our Need for Him

Psalm 119:50
My comfort in my suffering is this:
Your promise renews my life (NIV)

Prayer is not something reserved for dire predicaments, a certain position or place, or an activity we must begin or end with particular words. God is not someone we dial or e-mail. He is with us always. He has promised that and much more. We need to reach out to Him and sense His presence at all times. We need to know what He has promised and claim those promises for ourselves. The more we turn to Him, the more we learn we can trust Him. That kind of dependency does not come naturally for us. It takes practice.

Another of my family's favorite movies is *The Karate Kid*. The story is about a teenage boy with problems all too common to teenagers today: few friends, divorced parents, and picked on everywhere he turns. When he gets to know an old man who is a karate master, his life changes. The karate master promises to teach the youth karate, but only on the condition of the youth's absolute obedience. As the movie progresses and the youth spends hours polishing cars, the old master does not seem to be teaching the boy any karate. The boy doesn't see the point and is frustrated as he spends day after day applying wax and polishing the cars in the exact way the master demands. It is pointless torture to him. Later it becomes clear that those motions are the same movements the boy needed to block the bully's blows.

It is a wonderful metaphor for our relationship to God. God has made us promises, just as the karate master made promises. He also requires obedience, just as the karate master did. The boy could not experience the promises of the karate master overnight. In the process of his obedience, and with endless practice, making mistakes, relearning and more practice, the boy grew to be what the master had intended and promised. God's promise, that His grace is sufficient for us in any circumstance (2 Cor. 12:9), is also a process which we often do not recognize. While we are in the midst of suffering, we do not see how God is using it to mold our lives and strengthen our faith. Trusting in His promises in all circumstances is a learned process that often takes endless practice.

While the Bible is many things to us, it is also a manual that teaches us how to face suffering with joy. All how-to books have elements in common. Before they get started, they give an overview of what we will need and what is entailed. Then they start with step one and proceed, building step on step until the reader has achieved what was initially intended. If we don't do one of the steps properly, or if we skip a step, it won't come out right. When it fails, some people give up, but many go back, find what they did wrong, pick up from there and go on. Sometimes, they have to begin from the beginning.

The Bible teaches us through narrative and exhortation how we can trust God through suffering. We need to learn first of all to trust that God is who the Bible says He is, and that He can and will fulfill every promise He made. In short, our goal is to have perfect faith. The goal is achieved over time through a process or a series of steps. The necessary tools are a Bible and a heart that will allow the Holy Spirit to be heard as He teaches us.

The first step of the process is that we must understand we need Him, just like the youth turned to the karate master out of his need to defend himself. In the movie, the youth was repeatedly harassed and pulverized by bullies. His suffering led him to turn to the old karate master.

As Americans we don't like to admit we need help. We try to be self-sufficient and believe that as any need arises, people will always be able to find a solution. Most Americans have a very hard time admitting that they can't do something themselves. Those who recognize and accept their own weaknesses, and are not ashamed to call for help, generally suffer much less than those who are steadfast in their refusal to ask for help.

The quest for independence begins very early. I remember when one of our daughters was five or six months old and just starting on pureed food. Her food hit her cheek or chin or nose more than her mouth. What a mess! She would wail in frustration and bang her baby spoon on her highchair tray as food splattered in her hair, on the floor, everywhere. When I tried to help by guiding the spoon to her mouth, she clamped her lips, closed her eyes, and emphatically turned her head. She would rather starve than let me help her guide the spoon to her mouth.

Young children are notorious for wanting things their way and wanting to do things themselves. Toddlers aren't called "terrible twos" and "terrifying threes" for nothing. We parents often encourage the drive for independence. The toothpaste may be all over the counter, his clothes and his face, but he brushed his little teeth himself. His parents tell him how proud they are of his efforts. She may have gotten pink flowered shorts on backwards with an orange and yellow plaid shirt, but she picked out the clothes and dressed herself. Her parents chuckle at these first steps toward independence. They encourage more of it.

The twos and threes are bad, but the teenage years are worse. My father used to say that the goal of every teenager was to be five years older. The urge for independence, which begins as a trickle, reaches flood stage in puberty and adolescence. They don't want help. They don't want advice. They do not want to be dependent! My father often mused how wonderful life would be if only they would just lock all children up when they turned 12 and release them when they turned 20. Families who cling to God and remember His instructions for parents and children survive those years with the fewest scars.

Don't think this stubborn insistence on self-reliance is something we out-grow. It is a well known and documented fact that part of the male gene prohibits men from asking directions when they are driving someplace new. "Honey, we've been past this corner four times. There's a gas station." Ha. He won't stop and ask. Well, he might stop, but she has to ask.

I know there are women who routinely ask their husbands to help with arranging childcare, the laundry and grocery shopping. In 50+ years, I've only met a few. The phrases, "laundry impaired" and "grocery challenged" come to mind. I am as guilty as the next. I had a fever and a throat so sore that I cried every time I swallowed. I was up all night spraying my throat with an anesthetic. By morning I felt more dead than alive. Did I stay in bed and ask my beloved husband to get our son up and off to school? Did I ask him to throw a load of laundry in the washer before he left for work? No way, although he is perfectly capable of doing both. Me, admit I couldn't do it? We don't like to admit we need help.

To Show Us Our Need for Him

You have completed the first step when you recognize that without help you cannot conquer life's problems and trials. The second step is knowing where to turn. People mess up at this stage because they either do not know that there is someone there who can and will help, or they turn to the wrong source of help.

We learn first from our parents that someone will respond when we cry for help. Unfortunately, many families give their children the message that it is not okay to cry for help. Sometimes the message is delivered harshly, but often the family is just too busy or doesn't have the resources to help. Children from those families learn to be self-sufficient because they must.

We may not have any other resources, but we can always turn to God for help. We must teach our children that they can depend on God too.

Another problem people encounter is turning to the wrong place for help. Had the young man in *The Karate Kid* gone to his mother to help solve the problem of the kids picking on him, he never would have been able to defend himself. We don't call an electrician to fix a leaky faucet or a dentist to treat a broken toe. Yet, knowing where to turn for help is sometimes elusive.

Teenagers hate to turn to their parents for help. When they are in the midst of adolescent turmoil, struggling with understanding who they are and where they fit into the world, they are most likely to turn to their friends for help. How can friends, who are in the middle of their own turmoil, help the struggling teen? Wise children turn to parents or to other people who can show them God's perspective.

Confusion in where to turn for help in troubled times is common. When people are in a panic, they frequently grab at anything or anyone that is near or promises hope. Prisons are filled with drug dealers and con artists who got caught deceiving people into thinking they had the answers.

We must choose to turn to God for strength, for guidance, for courage, and for miracles. He is always there, wanting to help us. There we are, blind to our need, ignorant of the Source of help. If our parents have not taught us everyone's need for God, we must find Him on our own or through others. People who do not know God want something tangible, like another person, to turn to. By knowing and trusting God, we can feel his presence, as though another person is touching us.

Sometimes we don't start looking for help until we are suffering. God might let us suffer so that we *will* turn to Him. When we are doing well and life is flowing smoothly, we tend to forget the Lord and our need for Him. This is why Agur wrote,

> Keep deception and lies far from me,
> Give me neither poverty nor riches;
> Feed me with the food that is my portion,
> That I may not be full and deny *You* and say
> "Who is the Lord?" (Prov. 30:8-9).

We tend to forget God in our successes. It is when things are going badly, when we or those we love suffer and have no answers that we turn to God. God's relationship to the Israelites throughout the Old Testament illustrates our tendency to forget God when things are going well in our lives.

It began with their suffering as slaves in Egypt and crying out to God, which in itself, is remarkable. They were slaves four hundred years, surrounded by idol worshipers. They had no Bible to keep them together, no Mosaic Law and customs to unite them. All they had was God's promise made hundreds of years before and the sign of the covenant, given to their ancestor Abraham, in the circumcision of the Israelite boys. Had they not suffered, they would have had no reason to cry out to God.

They flourished under His protection and forgot that God was the reason they had flourished. Once they forgot their need, God removed His protection to let them suffer, and the cycle that began with blessing ended with suffering once again. The Book of Exodus is a beginning of the series of these cycles.

God *let* them suffer. The word "let" has two meanings that both apply. One can let something happen by simply standing aside and doing nothing to prevent the activity. When God removes His protection, He does that—stands aside and lets things take their course. Inevitably, without God's protection there is suffering in our lives.

There is another sense of "let," the sense of giving permission, allowing something to happen. A parent says, "I will let you take the car tonight." The teen is being given the opportunity to take the car.

God lets us suffer so we will choose to turn to Him in both cases. When the Israelites first refused to go into the Promised Land because they did not trust God to take care of them, He let them wander for 38 more years. Those extra years were not simply a punishment for not trusting God. During those extra 38 years of wandering the Israelites learned they could depend upon God. They learned to trust Him. He provided food, manna and quail. He provided water. Neither their clothes nor sandals wore out.

Those extra 38 years the Israelites suffered in the desert accomplished what was intended. When they again came to the land God had promised them, they trusted God to keep His promises and do whatever was necessary to give them the land. They knew they could not do it without God, and they knew God would provide.

God wants us to know that He is the one to turn to. Sometimes He will let us suffer to teach us that He is our help. The Book of Judges presents a series of the Israelites cycling out of belief and into suffering, crying out and being rescued, and rekindling their faith. Judges chapters 6-8 is just one such example. Chapter 6 opens with the Israelites suffering.

> Then the sons of Israel did what was evil in the sight of the Lord; and the Lord gave them into the hands of Midian seven years (6:1).

God removed His hedge of protection and allowed the Midianites and the Amalekites to swoop down like locusts from the mountains and destroy the Israelites' crops. These invaders left nothing for the Israelites or any of their animals for a period of seven years.

When they cried to the Lord, He told them that He had allowed it because, despite His having told them to have no fear of other gods, they had feared the gods of the Amorites. So God again set out to show them that with Him on their side they did not have to be afraid of anyone.

He chose Gideon to lead them. Gideon up until this time was not a remarkable person, just a regular guy. He was beating out wheat in the winepress to save it from the Midianites when an angel appeared to him. When Gideon saw the angel, like Moses, or probably like you or me, he thought God had made a mistake. He said, "O Lord, how shall I deliver Israel? Behold, my family is the least in Manasseh, and I am the youngest in my father's house" (Judg. 6:15).

Gideon, a man of wavering faith, asked God for proof that He really would deliver Israel through his leadership. He put

To Show Us Our Need for Him

a piece of fleece wool on the ground and asked the angel to make the fleece wet with all the land around it dry over night, and then make all the land around the wool wet with the fleece staying dry through the night. After Gideon was satisfied, God had Gideon break down the altars of Baal and Asherah that belonged to Gideon's father. God will not fight under any other god's banner or permit us to continue to follow other gods.

Gideon sent word to surrounding tribes for help in fighting the Midianites. Men came from Manasseh, Asher, Zebulun, and Naphtali. Too many men came.

> And the Lord said to Gideon, "The people who are with you are too many for Me to give Midian into their hands, for Israel would become boastful, saying, 'My own power has delivered me'" (Judg. 7:2).

God wants us to be as dependent on him as the Israelites were in the desert. He told Gideon to send home all but 300 men—300 men to fight an army as thick as a swarm of locusts. Gideon and his men followed God's plan and outwitted the entire Midianite army.

The first two steps to having joy in all of life's circumstances and suffering is to recognize our need and know to turn to God. We must daily acknowledge our need for God, and let Him work in our lives.

The story of Gideon serves as a great example, but also as a warning. God is eager to help us, but He does not when we forget our need for Him. The story of Gideon does not end with the defeat of the Midianites. The cycle of blessing and suffering began again. The Midianites had all worn earrings, and Gideon took one gold earring from each man's spoil. He melted down the gold and made a breastplate that God had said the priest was to wear. As happens all too often, their center of worship became not God who had delivered them, but the object they made to represent God (Judg. 8:24-27).

The instructions are clear: Love God with all your heart, mind, soul and strength. The promise is clear: He will turn all things to the good for those who love Him. The warning is clear: We must not deceive ourselves into thinking anything or anyone but God is the source of our strength and salvation.

We need to see that we fight the same cycle as the Israelites. America is a prime example. From the entire public speeches and writings of our founding fathers, it is apparent that our nation began as a God-fearing country. As we have become more powerful and prosperous, our country has become more ungodly. It is part of the human condition. We learn very little with just one lesson and we become expert at nothing without practice. Trusting God in all things, really trusting God takes practice. Trusting God is more difficult than playing in the Olympics and more rewarding than playing in the NBA. Over the course of a lifetime, how many hours does an Olympic athlete or professional basketball player practice? Innumerable!

The movie *Rocky* comes to mind. It is the story of a man who has drifted through life and buried his talent under a bushel. He is given a freak chance to fight against the current heavyweight boxing champion. Over the course of the movie we see him train. It is hard work, and it takes a long time. It is worth the pain and struggle for him because it gives him a chance to prove that he is somebody. That is his reward.

Rewards are important. The Olympic athlete makes a name for himself. Most NBA players get respect and a great deal of money. The kid in *The Karate Kid* learned to defend himself against anyone. Our reward is nothing less than

To Show Us Our Need for Him

experiencing the confidence and joy of which James spoke when he said, "Consider it all joy, my brethren, when you encounter various trials" (James 1:2).

That is our goal, to be able to face our trials with joy. Paul suffered from within and without. God allowed all that suffering to teach Paul to depend on Him, as He had taught the Israelites. Paul's understanding grew because of his suffering. He told the believers in Corinth that his personal suffering was necessary because God had allowed him a glimpse of heaven:

> Because of the surpassing greatness of the revelations, for this reason, to keep me from exalting myself, there was given me a thorn in the flesh, a messenger of Satan to torment me—to keep me from exalting myself! Concerning this I implored the Lord three times that it might leave me. And He has said to me, "My grace is sufficient for you, for power is perfected in weakness." Most gladly, therefore, I will rather boast about my weaknesses, so that the power of Christ may dwell in me. Therefore I am well content with weaknesses, with insults, with distresses, with persecutions, with difficulties, for Christ's sake; for when I am weak, then I am strong (2 Cor. 12:7-10).

Paul's understanding came through his suffering. He may have understood when he first felt his thorn that it's purpose was to keep him from becoming prideful. He might have said, "Okay, Lord. I felt the thorn. I know what you want of me. I can do that, keep from exalting myself. You can have Satan take it away now." Paul did not understand that the thorn had more than one purpose. One was to teach Paul he had a weakness and to keep him from exalting himself. The greater purpose was to show Paul his constant need for God.

Paul asked the Lord three times to remove his thorn. God did not remove it. What God gave Paul was worth much more than relief from Paul's unnamed "thorn." What God gave Paul enabled him to be content not only with his thorn, but with all the other abuse he describes in verse ten. Paul's Greek words of verse nine literally say, "Wherefore I am well pleased...." Not merely content, he was well pleased in his weaknesses because God had given him grace and power.

What God gave Paul and what God gives us is the understanding that His grace and His promises are enough to sustain us through anything. His promises are that He will work everything to the good for those who love Him, that we will have everlasting life with Him, that He will never depart from us. Those promises are what enable us also to be well pleased when we are suffering.

Faith does not just happen; it is developed. Each time the boy in *The Karate Kid* waxed a car he became stronger and his arms got used to the movements he would need to defend himself. Each time we suffer, turn to God, and find that He is there our faith and trust is strengthened. Each time Paul was mistreated or encountered difficulties, he found God's grace sufficient to help him through. By the time he wrote Second Corinthians, Paul knew God would always be with him. Like the Psalmist, Paul could have written, "My comfort in my suffering is this: Your promise renews my life" (Ps. 119:50, NIV).

That is what happened to Paul, and it can happen to us. The goal in needing God is to be complete in our faith. And it is possible to do just that as we find God through our various trials.

Chapter 7

To Make Us Like Jesus

Philippians 3:10
I want to know Christ and the power of his resurrection
and the fellowship of sharing in his sufferings,
becoming like him in his death (NIV)

What Would Jesus Do? WWJD. This password among Christians is a quick guide for us to monitor our behavior and our responses. Through Bible study we learn of Jesus' kindness and patience and purity and love, and we use those pictures to help us in our walk with Him. He was holy. We are told at least 24 times in the Old and New Testaments that we are to be holy because God is holy.

We are to be like Jesus, the image of God the Father. Paul says that we are "predestined to *become* conformed to the image of His Son, that He would be the firstborn among many brethren" (Rom. 8:29). We have descriptions of Jesus in the Gospels, and the writings of the apostles teach us what it means to be holy. We are to be holy in our day to day living as well as in our suffering. As Philippians 3:10 says, we need to become like Him even in our death, for death is part of life.

In Ecclesiastes we are told that suffering is part of this life. Jesus also told us that we must suffer when He said, "If anyone would come after me, he must deny himself and take up his cross daily and follow me" (Luke 9:23). Understanding why and how Jesus suffered will help us be more like Him, to take up our crosses daily and follow Him.

Why God Lets People Suffer

The first part of Paul's word in Philippians says, "I want to know Christ." One reason we want to know Christ's suffering is that He came down from heaven as a man to show us how to live as a child of God. Jesus is our role model. When we learn how Jesus responded to suffering, we will learn how to reflect Him in the hard times of our lives. As Peter wrote,

> For this *finds* favor, if for the sake of conscience toward God a person bears up under sorrows when suffering unjustly. For what credit is there if, when you sin and are harshly treated, you endure it with patience? But if when you do what is right and suffer *for it* you patiently endure it, this *finds* favor with God. For you have been called for this purpose, since Christ also suffered for you, *leaving you an example for you to follow in His steps* [italics mine] (1 Pet. 2:19-21).

Once we get to know Jesus and understand His suffering, we will know that through suffering He experienced the power of the Holy Spirit, the same Holy Spirit who helps us in our suffering. We will know that Jesus understands our pain. He suffered greater pain than most of us will ever know. He understands whatever pain we may have to suffer. We will know we are not alone.

All of us who believe understand that Jesus suffered and died to take upon Himself the sins of the world that we may share in His righteousness. He also learned from that suffering what is probably the hardest lesson for all of us—obedience. Jesus did not come on His own to save the world. John wrote, "And we have seen and testify that the Father has sent his Son to be the Savior of the world" (1 John 4:14). It was the will of our Father to save the world from its sin. And it was

His will that Jesus, His Son, come to earth as a baby and suffer life and death as a man. Jesus had to be obedient to our Father's will. To be obedient, we too must set aside our will and accept God's will. That is what Jesus did. The author of Hebrews tells us, "Although he was a Son, he learned obedience from what he suffered. . . " (Heb. 5:8). When we study Christ's suffering, we learn how to be obedient in our own times of travail. Learning obedience is not easy.

Jesus is our role model in suffering. People who are going through financial reverses and debilitating illnesses can look to Jesus, because Jesus too was humiliated and lost everything as a man. Can we even understand what it meant for Jesus to step out of His Godly realm and clothe Himself in human flesh? He was God, and He became human. He came to earth as a baby. Babies don't get much dignity and respect. They are wholly dependent. He could have begun His time on earth as a fully-grown, powerful king. He could have come to earth at the moment He started His ministry and dispensed with the painful processes of growing to maturity. Yet, He chose to come as a baby in the family of a simple carpenter.

Jesus was God, yet He chose to live as a humble servant of His Father God. Regardless of our station in life, we, too, are called to be humble servants of God, even as Jesus humbled Himself to become a man. We are to depend upon God and walk humbly with Him. And we are to do justice and love, grace and mercy, righteousness and kindness (Micah 6:8). It's as if God said, "I told you through Moses and through all of my prophets and you still don't get it. I will come Myself and show you." Jesus lived with the heart attitude we must all seek.

He came to show us that the things the world values—physical abilities, money, good looks, charisma, talent, and power—will all come to nothing. Still, it is hard to lose them once we have had them. It is difficult to focus on God and not on the qualities and things this world says are important.

I know. I like jewelry, well, not jewelry per se. I loved two bracelets I had that were my grandmother's. One she gave me was silver filigree with three tiny garnets. It wasn't worth much in dollars, but it meant a lot to me. The other one was gold with my grandmother's initials on it, which she wore long before she married my grandfather. And there were pearls, gold and diamonds, all kept in a little box at the very back of the drawer in my bathroom.

I cried when I realized someone had stolen my jewelry. It hurt because my grandmother's bracelets weren't replaceable. Then I remembered Jesus' words, "Do not store up for yourselves treasures on earth, where moth and rust destroy, and where thieves break in and steal" (Matt. 6:19). They had not stolen my memories of my grandmother. They had only stolen things, just as the Lord had warned. Things can seem so important, but they're not. The Lord was born a baby in a simple carpenter's family to show us that we don't need things.

Jesus teaches us how we are to respond to such losses. He was humiliated far beyond what most of us must endure. It is hard when people lose their jobs and lose their possessions. Many people each year are so debt-ridden they declare bankruptcy, and that is hard too. People who were once healthy and independent find themselves dependent on family, the government, and charity. At times life may even seem too hard to bear. But Jesus went before us. Keeping our eyes on Him will help us triumph in spite of any loss.

Jesus lost His honor and prestige among men. I know no one who has attained more respect than Jesus did during his lifetime. Jesus entered Jerusalem for the last time over roads

TO MAKE US LIKE JESUS

crowded with multitudes worshiping Him, crying, "Blessed is the King who comes in the name of the Lord; Peace in heaven and glory in the highest!" (Luke 19:38). No one today gets that kind of honor.

He entered the city knowing the suffering that would follow. He knew what would happen in the next few days as surely as a person who is diagnosed with a terminal illness knows what his future will be. Jesus knew the humiliation and pain He was to suffer, and it caused him great anguish. Yet, He was still obedient. By studying Jesus' suffering we learn how to be obedient as victims of unjust suffering too.

We cannot say anyone deserves to live a life in a wheelchair, or deserves to be homeless and desolate. We cannot say anyone deserves to have a child die or go astray, or have an abusive parent or spouse. It isn't a question of deserving. Jesus did not deserve to be stripped, beaten, spat upon, and then ridiculed as He hung on a cross. We study Jesus' suffering to learn how He reacted in the face of life's harsh realities, and how we also are to endure suffering.

In the final week of His earthly life, Jesus entered Jerusalem knowing He would die. Yet He faced crucifixion not alone, but in God's hands. Thoughts of His impending death undoubtedly occupied His mind as He and the apostles prepared the Passover meal, the Seder. The Seder is much more than a meal. It is foremost a family worship service. God commanded the Israelite parents to tell their children every year throughout all generations of how God had brought their ancestors out of Egypt and made them a nation (Ex. 12: 21-27). The Seder is a remembrance, and the whole family participates, even the youngest child.

But on this night Jesus used the common elements of bread and wine to tell them once again—though they hardly understood—that He was going to die; and that the breaking of His body and the shedding of His blood for their sins was to be remembered forever by their sharing of these elements together. Jesus faced His suffering with faith. He was glad to lay down His life for His friends of every age (John 15:12-15).

The twelve apostles were family to Jesus. They were like brothers and like sons to Him. He even called them His children at the Passover dinner when He told them He would be going where they could not come (John 13:33). They lived with Him for three years. He loved them—even Judas Iscariot—as He loves us. He told them, "A new commandment I give to you, that you love one another, even as I have loved you, that you also love one another" (John 13:34).

The apostles were not like the crowds to Jesus. He knew that the crowds who had worshiped Him as He entered Jerusalem could easily be swayed against Him. Any person who has been in the public favor (politicians, actors, sports stars) knows that crowds are fickle. They are all for you until something else comes along. The apostles were different. He had allowed them to get close, to be part of His ministry and part of His life.

Jesus knows what it is like to have those you most love turn on you. Judas betrayed Jesus, but Judas was not the only one. When He was arrested in Gethsemane, all the apostles fled (Mark 14:50). Peter denied that he knew Jesus three times (Mark 14:66-72). His brothers did not believe in Him (John 7:5). He even understands the hurt of having his Father turn His back. Just before He died, with the sins of the whole world on His shoulders, He cried out, "My God, My God, why have you forsaken me?" (Mark 15:34). God cannot coexist with sin, so He had to turn His back on His own Son at that moment. And Jesus was all alone. He understands your devastation.

We know from the Gospels of Mark, Matthew and Luke

that Jesus' foreknowledge of what He was to suffer did not make His suffering any easier. In these Gospels we are told that in Gethsemane Jesus said that His soul was deeply grieved to the point of death, and He asked God to take from Him the cup, the suffering that Jesus knew would follow (see Mark 14:34-36). Luke reports that Jesus was in such agony, that as He was praying fervently "His sweat came like drops of blood" (Luke 22:44).

He knew the physical torture and humiliation to come. He had to be prepared to endure what God had ordained. In preparing Himself, He taught us how to prepare for our ordeals. Pray. Pray fervently. Pray, trusting God to strengthen you and to work all things, even that which you must suffer, to the good. Pray, being strengthened by the knowledge that whatever you are going through, Jesus has already experienced your pain.

Jesus knew His Father's plan. He knew what He was supposed to do, how long it would last and that the salvation of mankind rested on His being obedient. Ultimately He trusted our Father enough to endure and play His part in God's plan. The Gospels tell us that Jesus ended his prayer by telling God that He would do His will (Matt. 26:42, Mark 14:36, Luke 22:42). Jesus needed an angel from heaven to strengthen him just before He was arrested (Luke 22:43).

In addition to prayer and obedience, suffering teaches us how we are to react to unjust suffering. In Matthew we learn that Jesus was bound and led away in the middle of the night to Caiaphas for a sort of trial. There they tried to find false witnesses to frame Him even though He was blameless. There they spat in His face and beat him with their fists and slapped Him.

The next day they took Jesus to Pilate, the Roman governor, and after Pilate agreed to let Barabbas go in exchange for

Jesus, He was whipped and stripped of His robe. They embedded a crown of thorns in His head and mocked Him. Again they spat on Him and beat Him before they put His clothes back on and led Him away to be crucified (see Matt. 26 and 27).

Whenever I read about His suffering and humiliation, I want Jesus to say, "That's enough!" He was God and could have killed them with a thought. In my flesh, I want Him to do just that. It's like our son. On the way to the bus stop he was grousing about another boy and telling me what he was going to say to him if the boy was at the bus stop. I asked him, "WWJD?"

He said, "Jesus would do just what I'm going to."

I asked, "How can you say that? Look at how He lived and commanded us to forgive?"

Our son answered, "'Vengeance is *mine*!' said the Lord!"

That's what I wish Jesus would have done to those who were persecuting Him. But He didn't because He is God's Son and He came as a role model for us. Jesus suffered in silence. Only the Holy Spirit could get us to endure with silence someone spitting at us, beating us, humiliating us.

There is a silence when there is nothing to say and a defiant silence when someone refuses to answer. Jesus' silence was neither of these. Isaiah tells us,

> He was oppressed and He was afflicted,
> Yet He did not open His mouth;
> Like a lamb that is led to slaughter,
> And like a sheep that is silent before its shearers,
> So did He not open His mouth (Is. 53:7).

Jesus' silence was one of acceptance. He accepted the painful part He was to play in God's plan for our salvation.

He was obedient because He trusted God, our Father. We, too, can accept the suffering God allows in our lives with the help of the Holy Spirit. Pray, and He will help us trust God too.

The account of the crucifixion in Mark is nearly identical to that in Matthew, but in Luke we see more of Christ on the cross and learn three important lessons of how we are to respond as we suffer. First, we are to forgive and ask God to forgive those who unjustly abuse us. Jesus said, "Father, forgive them; for they do not know what they are doing" (Luke 23:34).

If we are certain we are being unjustly treated, we can learn to forgive by believing God's promises. God *will* work all things to the good for those who love Him. God has also promised to avenge wrongs against us, because wrongs against His saints are sins against Him. When Samuel was unhappy that the Israelites wanted a king over them, not another judge, God comforted Samuel when He told him,

> "Listen to the voice of the people in regard to all that they say to you, for they have not rejected you, but they have rejected Me from being king over them" (1 Sam. 8:7).

The Gospels quote Jesus telling His disciples that they were not to fight back when people were unkind to them. He told them that for those who don't welcome them or listen to them, they are to shake the dust off their feet as they leave for a testimony against them (Mark 6:11). You can trust that God will keep His promise to punish those who abuse His saints. He tells us both in Deuteronomy, "Rejoice, O nations, with His people; for He will avenge the blood of His servants" (32:43); and in Romans, "Never take your own revenge, beloved, but leave room for the wrath *of God*, for it is written, 'Vengeance is Mine, I will repay,' says the Lord" (Rom. 12:19).

We, too, can say, "Father, please forgive them, they don't

know what they are doing," because we know that God will punish them.

The other two lessons we learn from Christ on the cross in Luke are contained in the exchange between Jesus and one of the other two men being crucified. While one criminal joined in the ridicule of Jesus, the other told the first to stop because Jesus was innocent. Then he asked Jesus to remember him when Jesus got to His kingdom (Luke 23:41-42). How did he know Jesus was innocent, that He was of God and going to His kingdom? We fully explore the answer in chapter 10; but simply, the second criminal came to faith by watching Jesus during His ordeal. The lesson for us is that others will be brought to faith by seeing God's strength and truth in us when we suffer unjustly.

There is still one lesson to learn from Jesus' crucifixion. Jesus was whipped, spat upon, stripped, humiliated, mocked, beaten, and crucified. Even as He was dying, people were ridiculing Him. Yet, Jesus took the time and energy to comfort the criminal who asked to be remembered. He turned to him and said, "Truly I say to you, today you shall be with Me in Paradise" (Luke 23:43).

Our pain should not keep us from being God's servants or from ministering to others. We are not allowed, by Jesus' example, to be so wrapped up in our own suffering that we take no heed of others' needs.

My former mother-in-law, Margaret, taught me this aspect of Christlikeness many years ago when I was a recent widow from my second marriage. My first husband's parents had become family to me in the nearly 14 years before their son had left me. My former father-in-law was very sick and hospitalized with a terminal illness in a distant city. It would not have been surprising if Margaret had been so absorbed with her husband's illness and pain and her impending loss

To Make Us Like Jesus

that she would have taken no notice of my visit.

Both of my first husband's parents were committed Christians. In the midst of her pain, watching her beloved husband die a little each day, she took the time and energy, just like Jesus, to come downstairs and visit with me. She was most concerned with the recent death of my second husband and how we were coping. She comforted me and worried about helping us. That is how we are to behave in the midst of our suffering.

Jesus knows what it is like to be rejected. He understands what it is like to go from the top of the heap to being alone, despised and ridiculed. He can understand your pain. With the help of the Holy Spirit, you too can have the faith, trust and courage to say, "Thy will be done," when it is your time to suffer. We know that Jesus can understand our pain, and that we are to accept our suffering, trusting God to work all things to the good for those who love him.

Daily we may face trials. Daily we must be ready and willing to follow Jesus' example. When we are faced with crosses, we can choose how to react. We can try to deny we have a cross to bear in a Pollyanna like fashion. We can try to avoid our crosses, but that is like taking a bad shortcut. We can grumble about our suffering, as if complaining ever helped a situation. We can resent having to suffer and let our cross turn us against God. If we do, we will have forgotten Jesus as our role model.

There is another choice. We can accept our suffering as Jesus did, as part of God's plan for our lives to make us more like our Savior. His Spirit gives us the strength to accept the suffering, to pray, to ask forgiveness for those who wrong us, and to minister to others in the midst of our suffering. We do not have to do it on our own. Every day He gives us the strength and faith to endure our suffering.

Chapter 8

That We May Comfort Others

> *2 Corinthians 1:3-4*
> The God of all comfort . . . comforts us in all our troubles, so that we can comfort those in any trouble with the comfort we ourselves have received from God (NIV)

People have asked me to tell them the one reason they were suffering, but often that would seem to be limiting God. In a single period of suffering God allows into our lives, He might be accomplishing several purposes at once. We see this in what the Israelites learned during their four hundred years of slavery.

In the years between Israel's (first called Jacob) death at the end of Genesis to the escape from Egypt in Exodus, the Israelites went from an honored family to a multitude of slaves. The descendants of Abraham were chosen by God to be His people, yet He allowed them to be slaves for four hundred years, just as He had told Abraham (Gen. 15:13).

Israelite slavery was not without purpose. God did three great things during their oppression and rescue. First, He created a nation. Second, through His rescue, God revealed three aspects of His character. Third, God taught the Israelites compassion through their own suffering.

The creation of the nation of Israel did not happen overnight, and really began with God's calling of Abraham, roughly six hundred years before the Exodus. Through Abraham God promised to build a nation, a people called to holiness in service to Him and ministry to the world. They were to be set apart by customs and law—by the ways they treated each other and their fellow human beings. Most of all, they were to be a people who worshiped the God of their fathers, and He alone.

It might seem that a godly culture would not take six hundred or even four hundred years to establish in holiness, faith and power. Yet even though we know little about the Hebrew people during their years of servitude in Egypt, it is not likely that their living habits set them apart too much from other people of their world. They did not yet have the Mosaic Law, which has set Jews apart since the Exodus. This is not to say they were without laws or faith, for they did cry to God—not idols—for deliverance.

The Israelites were partially set apart by geography. Joseph originally settled his family in the area of Egypt called Goshen, where they stayed. When God rained hail on Egypt, "Only in the land of Goshen, where the sons of Israel were, there was no hail" (Ex. 9:26). Yet they weren't the only people living in Goshen, the land in Egypt's north delta country along the Nile. Goshen was not just a slave ghetto, for the Bible tells us that the Israelites had Egyptian neighbors who gave them silver and gold and clothing when they left Egypt (Ex. 3:21-22, 12:35-36).

But there were three distinguishing characteristics of the Israelites which definitely set them apart from their Egyptian neighbors: (1) their language (2) their belief in one God, and (3) circumcision. All three characteristics would be further developed through the giving of the Mosaic Law and the settlement in Canaan as Israel began to bond into a cohesive nation.

Although the Hebrew language was not fully developed until after the conquest, a Semitic dialect similar to Hebrew was likely spoken in Egypt. This would have set them apart, even as people who are bilingual in America are different.

The most notable difference between Israelites and Egyptians was Israel's monotheism. Nearly all ancient cultures were heavily idolatrous, and Egypt was no exception. Gods represented every facet of nature. Fear and superstition ruled the thoughts and actions of human beings everywhere. But not so the Israelites, who shared the faith of their father Abraham that one God was the creator and ruler of the universe. This was a God to be worshiped, not feared as an unknown deity and manipulated.

Circumcision, given to Abraham as a symbol of God's covenant promises, was the ultimate physical sign of Israel's monotheism. Circumcision not only separated the Hebrews from their Egyptian neighbors, it set them apart for God as a sign of their obedience and a reminder to cry out to the God of their ancestors.

Further, circumcision of the flesh was a sign of inner faith. Circumcision of the *heart* is shown by our obedience and has separated God's children from the rest of the world since the time of Abraham.

Although the Israelites knew they were a people set apart to worship and serve the God of Abraham, Isaac, and Jacob, they were still enslaved and oppressed. Their only hope was in the God of their ancestors, and He delivered them. When we are oppressed, as children of God, we too know that our hope is in Him.

Through the rescue of the Hebrew slaves, God was not only creating a nation, but He also taught them three aspects of His character which would guide them in the years ahead. The first is that God's *time* is not our time. To us four hundred years seems like an eternity. Four hundred years is twenty generations. God knew it would take four hundred years of slavery for the Israelites to become a people with no hope except for Him. He heard them when they cried out to Him (Ex. 2:23-24). I do not believe they were slaves one day longer than they needed to be. Had they lived a life of ease and luxury in Egypt, few would have followed—or even heard—God's calling to the uncertainties of Canaan. But four hundred years of slavery well prepared their hearts to leave. Four hundred years isn't long in God's time. Four hundred years compared to eternity is nothing. An important characteristic of God is that His time has an eternal perspective, while ours does not.

The second characteristic is that God is *able* to keep His promises. Only God could redeem the Israelites from slavery in Egypt. To convince the Egyptians to let them go, He had to prove to them that He alone was God and that He alone controlled the universe. The Egyptian magicians tried to keep up with God, but only God could revoke His own plagues (Ex. 7-12). The Egyptians and Israelites learned that "Nothing is impossible with God" (Luke 1:37, NIV). When the world seems out of control, remember that God is able.

The third characteristic God taught the Hebrew people is that He *will* keep His promises. The Israelites learned from their slavery and rescue that God is faithful. That the Israelites knew to circumcise their sons and knew to cry out to God shows that they had been told of Abraham's God and His promises. That they cried out to God and followed Moses indicates they believed those promises. God is faithful to us in His promises too. Even when all seems hopeless, when it seems God cannot possibly keep His promise, God finds a way. To the slaves, freedom in their own land seemed impossible. To accomplish that, God had to convince the Egyptians to let the Israelites go, and He had to get the Israelites and all who accompanied them safely across the Sea of Reeds

That We May Comfort Others

(also called the Red Sea). Then He had to sustain this multitude of people in the Sinai Desert until they reached the Land of Promise.

> Now the sons of Israel journeyed from Ramses to Succoth, about six hundred thousand men on foot, aside from children. A mixed multitude also went up with them, along with flocks and herds, a very large number of livestock (Ex. 12:37-38).

It seemed impossible for God to be able to keep all His promises to Abraham. But He did. It is as important today for us to know God's promises to us as it was for the Israelites to know what God had promised them through Abraham. God rescued them after they cried out to Him. Throughout the Bible, God has made promises to everyone who believes and trusts in Him, promises that He keeps when we come to Him in faith.

Knowing those promises and trusting that God will keep them enables us to endure the suffering we face. Knowing who they were and learning that God could and would keep His promises in His time enabled the Israelites to follow God. Yet, that was not all the Israelites were to have learned from those hundreds of years of slavery. They also needed to learn compassion for others.

The Israelites' story is our story. For many of us, the biggest difference between the Israelites' experience and our own is that the Israelites knew they were children of God's promise and knew they were slaves. We in the family of God are a people no less than the Israelites were. Like the Israelites, we who believe in Jesus are a people, a family, a body. We are to be one body. As Paul said,

> For by one Spirit we were all baptized into one body, whether Jews or Greeks, whether slaves or free, and we were all made to drink of one Spirit. For the body is not one member, but many (1 Cor. 12:13-14).

We believers, like the Israelites, are a people, and we, like the Israelites, were slaves before God rescued us. Without God, we are all slaves to our own nature. For those who doubt that our nature is sinful, consider that parents never have to teach their children to be selfish or mean. They must teach their children to be nice. God has just as surely saved us from the yoke of slavery to our natural instincts as He saved the Israelites from their slavery to Pharaoh. As Paul wrote to Titus,

> For we also once were foolish ourselves, disobedient, deceived, enslaved to various lusts and pleasures, spending our life in malice and envy, hateful, hating one another. But when the kindness of God our Savior and *His* love for mankind appeared, He saved us, not on the basis of deeds which we have done in righteousness, but according to His mercy, by the washing of regeneration and renewing by the Holy Spirit, whom He poured out upon us richly through Jesus Christ our Savior (Titus 3:3-6).

We, too, were slaves, just like the Israelites. Who among us can say we did not succumb to the power of pride, of anger, or of lusts for food, or sex or wealth before we knew God? That the Holy Spirit enables us to break the bonds of those taskmasters is as much a miracle as God's parting the Sea of Reeds. We, too, are to learn compassion though our suffering. God wants us to use the experience of suffering that He has allowed in our lives to enable us to help others.

He told the Israelites,

> "And you shall not oppress a stranger, since you yourselves know the feelings of a stranger, for you *also* were strangers in the land of Egypt" (Ex. 23:9).

They had been strangers and the Lord brought them out. The experience in Egypt enabled the Israelites to understand what strangers and aliens and slaves felt. The Israelites were told twice in Exodus (22:21, 23:9), again in Leviticus (19:34), and yet again in Deuteronomy (10:19) that because they had been strangers in Egypt they should know what it felt like to be strangers. Because they knew what it felt like, they were commanded to have compassion and help those in the same situation from which God had rescued them.

Through suffering and the experience of God's faithfulness we learn to comfort others. As Paul said, "We can comfort those in any trouble with the comfort we ourselves have received from God" (2 Corinthians 1:4). Paul knew the comfort and deliverance he received and how he comforted others as a result of his own suffering. By unruly mobs and plotting men he was driven from Damascus (Acts 9:23-30), Pisidian Antioch (Acts 13:50), Iconium (Acts 14:5-6), Lystra (Acts 14:19), and Thessalonica (Acts 17:5-10). He was dragged into court in Corinth (Acts 18:12-17). He was mobbed, beaten, and repeatedly tried in Jerusalem (see Acts 21:27 through 26:32). And he was shipwrecked on the way to Rome (Acts 27:9-44). Precisely because he had gone through all that persecution for proclaiming his faith, he was able through his letters to encourage others who were facing the challenge of false teaching and persecution.

We can best comfort others who are going through something we have already endured. When I am having trouble with a child, I do not want to hear advice from someone who is childless. I am so relieved when I encounter someone who can say, "I've been through that. Let me help you." We know from our earlier study of Jesus' suffering that He does that for us. No matter what we go through, He whispers, "I understand. I will comfort you."

There is nothing we can go through that Jesus did not already endure. Are you homeless? He was homeless (Matt. 8:19-20). Are you friendless? All of His friends deserted Him. Peter even denied he knew Him (Matt. 26:69-75). Are you picked on or persecuted? He was persecuted to death. Is your heart broken because your child has turned his back on all you taught him, all you believe in? We are God's children. He taught us through His Word and through His coming. Yet, we all turn our backs on Him sometimes. As Isaiah wrote, "All of us like sheep have gone astray, each of us has turned to his own way" (Is. 53: 6). We all fall short, even the great Apostle Paul: "For the good that I want, I do not do; but I practice the very evil that I do not want" (Rom. 7:19). God understands your heartbreak when your children stray.

God, our Father, watched as His Son was humiliated, tortured and killed. He did not stop it because He knew it was the only way to reconcile sinful mankind to Himself. We are not told about the Father's anguish, but we know how He felt about His Son. When Jesus was baptized, and again at the Transfiguration on the mountain God said, "This is my Beloved Son, in Whom I am well-pleased" (Matt. 3: 17, 17: 5). For those of you who have had a child suffer and for all those who have had a child die, let our Father comfort you. He knows how you feel.

He even understands when you are overwhelmed or just plain tired. He comforts me all the time. There are days that the whole day seems like a struggle. Then I remember that the

Lord got tired too. Once the word got out that He could heal the sick, the multitudes followed Jesus everywhere. He managed to escape from them from time to time, just to rest. He understands that we all need rest. He promised all of us,

> "Come to Me, all who are weary and heavy-laden, and I will give you rest. Take My yoke upon you, and learn from Me, for I am gentle and humble in heart, and you will find rest for your souls" (Matt. 11:28-29).

When I am overwhelmed and I remember this promise, I am comforted. Then I give myself permission to withdraw for a while to rest in God.

There is no sorrow we must bear that God has not already endured. Because we know He understands, He can comfort us. With the comfort we receive from knowing Jesus' life and promises, we can comfort and counsel others who come to us beaten down by the pressures of this world.

I have had a soap opera type life, but in all that I have suffered, God has sustained me and enabled me to help others. Because I nearly died in a car accident, I am able to help others who face death. Because I lost three children by miscarriage and nearly lost a son just before he turned two, I have been able to comfort others who have lost children. I counsel people who have been persecuted and ridiculed for their faith. I help people who have been neglected by their parents, those who suffered abuse as children, and those who have been made to feel worthless by their spouses. I help victims of divorce and custody battles and people who have lost a spouse. I help those whose children have gone astray and those who have loved ones hopelessly ill. I help people who have a loved one go to jail and those who have gone from financial success to ruin. Because God has been faithful throughout the suffering of my life, I can comfort others, and I am thankful.

Yet, comforting others with what we have been through is not all that God wants of us. We must take our compassion a step further. It is not enough to restrict ourselves to helping people who are struggling with something through which God has brought us. We are to imagine what it would be like to suffer what others suffer and then help them. God tells us,

> Remember the prisoners, as though in prison with them, *and* those who are ill-treated, since you yourselves also are in the body (Heb. 13:3).

It is not because we, ourselves, are suffering, but because we are in the body that we are to feel for others as if we were going through what they are going through. Whatever hurts another hurts us too. As John Donne (1572-1631) wrote,

> No man is an island, entire of itself; every man is a piece of the continent, a part of the main. If a clod be washed away by the sea, Europe is the less. . . . Any man's death diminishes me, because I am involved in mankind. . . .
>
> -Devotions XVII

Only the Israelites actually born in slavery were saved from slavery. Yet, God commanded every generation of Israelites to celebrate the Passover as if they themselves were redeemed (Ex. 12:42, 13:8). Whenever God sustains another in need, He has sustained us too. We will pray with one another in our suffering and rejoice with one another in our salvation. We will comfort others with the comfort we have received from God. Remembering that we can use our suffering to comfort others will help us face our suffering with the strength and peace that only comes from the comfort we have received from God.

Chapter 9

To Bring Others to Faith Through God's Work

John 11:45
Therefore many of the Jews who came to Mary and saw what He had done, believed in Him

It makes a difference to know my suffering is part of God's plan. Peace that surpasses human understanding (Phil. 4:7) is the fulfilled promise that comes in knowing our suffering has a heavenly purpose, one of which is to bring people to faith. There are two ways people can be brought to faith through our suffering. This chapter discusses how others can be brought to faith through witnessing God's work in our lives. Chapter 10 is about those who are brought to faith through our own testimony of faith in our suffering.

The knowledge that our suffering has a heavenly purpose does not remove the pain. Suffering is still suffering. But the peace that comes with trusting God enables us to endure. If you have ever been part of or witnessed a miracle, you know this is true.

I have a friend who has suffered greatly. His Marine Corps training helps explain his behavior throughout his affliction. As a Marine Corps Vietnam veteran in his late 50s, he had been well trained. He had learned not to analyze or deal with obstacles which were merely to be conquered. As a marine he'd learned to just keep pushing. Officers were to be obeyed without question. That they were officers meant that they were qualified. Their personalities and expertise were irrelevant.

Two years ago when his mother was ill, his feet began to go numb at unpredictable times. He went over to see her twice a day. It was a very stressful time. Over the course of the year, as her condition worsened and his care of his mother increased, his numbness also increased. The numbness and tingling and pain were as though his feet were asleep. Over the course of a year, the numbness moved up into his legs, then his trunk and arms. Bit by bit, his body weakened and he felt fatigued.

The doctors diagnosed it as peripheral neuropathy. Peripheral neuropathy is a condition in which nerve endings become coated so that the messages get garbled or cannot get through at all. It is most common in diabetics. But he was not a diabetic. He took prescribed medicines known to be effective for containing that disease, but his condition continued to worsen. His frustration grew.

Throughout his illness, he left the questioning of doctors to his wife. As a marine, doctors were like officers, so he did not question them. He kept his thoughts to himself, that they were just practicing, both on his mother and on him. It seemed plausible that his otherwise inexplicable bouts of numbness and pain could be side effects of the stress from his mother's illness. So as her condition and his condition both worsened, he just kept pushing. He would not allow himself to give in or give up, even when it became a struggle to do the simplest things, like walk down a hall without bumping into walls.

His mother died about a year after the episodes of numbness had begun. He thought his physical condition would get better, but his symptoms continued to worsen. He began falling down without apparent reason.

TO BRING OTHERS TO FAITH THROUGH GOD'S WORK

My friend and his wife had been Christians for a long time before all this began. Despite the pain and frustration with the doctors, they were at peace because they knew they were in God's hands. They did not know God's plan, but knew this suffering had a place in it, somehow. Still, against the background of peace, frustration occasionally erupted. He said, "I knew enough not to get mad at God, and I wouldn't let that happen. So sometimes I got angry, but I didn't know at whom. It was confusing. For the most part, though, there was no anger at all."

The summer after his mother died, the numbness and shooting pain had extended from his feet to his legs and to his hips. His only relief was in moving. Sitting was better than lying down. He could not lie in one position for more than a few seconds before the shooting pain began again. Sleeping was impossible. Fatigue was ever present. He began to use a cane. Happiness left him as he lost his strength.

At the end of July he went with his wife to a conference in New Mexico. There he began working with preschoolers, trying to regain his lost joy. On a spiritual level, he could not see God's purpose in his suffering. On a human level, if he had what the doctors said, the medicines should have stopped his deterioration. But they didn't. His illness made no sense. At the conference, there were times he wanted to fight, to hurt somebody, anybody. He never did. His wife felt an overwhelming sadness. She watched her husband painfully deteriorate and was unable to help him.

The preschoolers brought him temporary joy. As July gave way to August, his condition continued to worsen. When he couldn't swallow, they hospitalized him to stretch his esophagus. "Life seemed like Dante's Inferno. The world was dark. I couldn't see details of people, only vague images, seen through pain. It was hopeless. There was nothing they could do." Like Job, he had comforters. They did not try to point out his guilt, as Job's comforters had done. Instead, they quoted scripture about having joy in his suffering. They were annoying, not comforting. The comfort my friend and his wife received was from God and needed no human words.

The deterioration escalated throughout September. One cane was no longer enough for him to keep his balance. He began to use two canes. They laugh now when they remember disagreeing about his need to have matching canes. The marine in him would not allow him to give in to his overwhelming fatigue or his pain. Throughout September, despite his lack of sleep and his constant pain, he went to work every day.

As a maintenance supervisor, he often had to climb ladders and balance on high beams and rooftops. Surely God's angels steadied him there, for on earth he could not walk without the use of his canes. He also began to get lost, even at home. At the end of September he was sent to a clinic for sleep disorders, but he didn't have a sleep disorder. He had real pain that would not allow him to rest or sleep. Over the course of August and September, his facial features changed. At times, parts of his face drooped, as if he had had a stroke. At times he looked nearly unrecognizable, even ugly.

The end of September he inexplicably fell off a chair while working in a preschool class, and it was decided he could no longer work with children. That was when his wife let the people of their church know they needed prayer. Elders, pastors, and regular members of the church began to pray for them. Those prayers made a difference. It is a ploy of the evil one to make us think we must bear our burdens alone. They experienced a tremendous relief when they shared their burdens and knew others were praying with and for them. From this point on, they felt strengthened by all those prayers. During this time when they felt they could cry, they didn't. The prayers supported them, like giant arms surrounding them. Even when they thought they should get angry, they couldn't. The peace they experienced could only be described as supernatural. It was a peace that surpassed human understanding.

Early in October he was sent home from work because his legs could no longer hold him. He traded his two canes for a wheelchair. He felt like they took his life when they told him he could no longer drive. Through October he and his wife tried everything they could think of to bring him relief. Every day they had at least one appointment. They went to traditional doctors, to the VA hospital, to a chiropractor, and an acupuncturist. Nothing helped. They knew only God was sustaining him. That knowledge produced a peace that transcended the pain and frustration.

Then, at the very end of October, the pharmacologist at the VA hospital stopped them. He said my friend's condition could not be peripheral neuropathy. The medicines would have retarded the progression of that disease. The pharmacologist confirmed what his wife had found in her research, that the disease is extremely rare in nondiabetics, and they knew for certain he was not diabetic. Furthermore, the symptoms do not come and go in patients with peripheral neuropathy, as they did with him. The pharmacologist wanted to know why they had not seen a neurologist. They had been waiting to see the expert on peripheral neuropathy, who was out of the country until December. The pharmacologist told them they could not wait. They called their primary care doctor from the VA hospital. He arranged for them to get worked into a neurologist's office schedule on an emergency basis on Monday.

Why God Lets People Suffer

When they got to the neurologist's office, his nurse again told them he'd have to work them in, and she showed them to a room. The neurologist was furious at his nurse for allowing him an unscheduled appointment. They could hear him yelling at her through the door. In a practice with three of the five doctors unavailable, he was overworked and stretched farther than he thought possible already.

The doctor came into the room and explained that he could not see them. She replied that they were not leaving until someone looked at her husband. She had brought food and a change of clothes and could wait a long time.

God was clearly in control. Neither the primary care doctor nor my friend's file could be located, so the doctor could not see the other diagnosis and had to rely on his own, fresh observations. He looked at my friend's face, which now stayed in a stroke position, and looked into my friend's eyes, really peered into them. Then he ran out of the room and got his partner, who also peered into my friend's eyes.

Soon my friend and his wife were at the hospital, and he was being prepared for tests. The tests ruled out Parkinson's disease and other illnesses. The MRI told the story. There was a massive tumor covering the right side, the front and top of the brain. The doctor said it did not look good. It might not even be operable. The tests stopped for the day.

My friends were relieved to know, after two years of pain, what had caused all of their suffering. They understood only recently, when they finally got to see that first MRI. The doctor was right. It was massive. The tumor covered most of his brain.

IVs of steroids were begun immediately to shrink the swelling in the brain. The IVs left him confused. He felt like a human game piece in a game they couldn't play without him. He didn't understand and he doesn't remember much about his time in the hospital.

A pediatric neurosurgeon was called in because he was used to very small blood vessels and, if he could operate, they didn't know what web of arteries and veins attaching the tumor to the brain they would find. His type of tumor was called a gusher because it is typically full of blood.

The church and family and friends across the country were notified. The network of people praying grew. Every day men from the church came, circled his bed, and prayed for him. My friends felt God's presence. They also felt the relief that comes from knowing they were in God's hands.

The surgeon needed a second MRI and a CAT scan. Between the first and second MRI a miracle happened. The tumor had shrunk. It no longer covered the whole right side. It was no longer across the top or across the front at all. It had compressed into the right side. Everyone was astonished. They saw the two MRIs and knew they had just witnessed a miracle. The surgeon said, "We can get this one, but it's big."

The surgery was still very risky. It turned out that all the bad news was not in yet. On Friday, the doctors did an angioplasty. It is a procedure most commonly done in heart surgery to open arteries and veins. A balloon is inserted to temporarily shut off the blood supply while work can be done on the vein or artery. In his case, a balloon was inserted to shut off the blood supply to the tumor. In the course of performing the procedure, the doctor discovered there were not one, but two tumors. They were lined up side by side. He was able to shut off the blood supply to the tumor closest to the skull, but not to the tumor closest to the brain. To close off that blood supply would have risked shutting off the supply to that part of the brain as well.

Many people were touched by what happened to my friend. Between the time he entered the hospital and the surgery, he had had four different roommates. They and all the staff witnessed the miracle that had taken place between the two MRIs. They witnessed the peace that surrounded my friend and his wife as the quiet, spiritual music that his wife had brought played nonstop and as church members prayed in his room every day. He doesn't remember much about those days because of the steroids, but his wife remembers that he never lost his sense of humor. He took delight in the intern's constant banter. They made a game of asking him what day it was and what month. He teased them back, telling them that when they finally got out of school, they should buy themselves calendar watches. The nurses were wonderful. He remembers that they did a lottery for the honor of shaving his head for the surgery and teased that his was a $40,000 haircut. All of the nurses, aides, interns, residents, doctors and fellow patients witnessed the miracles.

One of the effects of the tumor was that he cried easily. When the surgeon called him a crybaby, he got mad. If he could have gotten out of bed and strangled the surgeon, he would have. He was still mad the day of the surgery. His wife insisted, "You can't go into surgery angry. This is the man God brought to save your life. You must forgive him. The Lord will not honor anger." So they prayed together. He gave God his anger and God gave him His peace once again.

They began to prepare him at 7 A.M. and made the first incision at 9:30. At 3:30 the doctor came out, shaking his head. "I got them. I got it all. He's doing fine, but it's the largest tumor I have ever removed from a living person. I have never seen anything this big."

The story of the miracles unfolded. When the surgeon removed the skull plate, the first tumor literally fell out into his hand. He set it aside and went to work on the tumor that was still attached to the brain. To his astonishment, it was only attached by a single blood vessel, which he easily clipped. The second tumor fell into his hand. Each tumor was the size of a baseball.

So many miracles had taken place. It was a miracle my friend was even alive with two tumors squeezing the life out of his brain. There was the miracle of the compression of the tumor that made it operable. And there were the miracles in surgery. Tumors are typically connected by a myriad of blood vessels and do not fall out of skulls. The entire surgical staff and attending staff witnessed the miracle during the surgery.

His immediate recovery was no less of a miracle. My friend spent only two hours in recovery and less than 24 hours in Intensive Care. Three days after surgery he was sent to a hospital specializing in rehabilitation of stroke victims.

Their suffering is not over. Complete recovery takes a long time after so much pressure has been put on the brain over such a long period of time. The miracles God performed with those tumors in my friend are a witness of His power. When my friend is able to drive, he will return to the hospital to talk to the doctors, interns, nurses and aides whose lives were changed by those miracles. My friends are learning how God touched others when He showed His power through them.

This is just one example from today's world of God allowing people to suffer to bring others to faith through witnessing His power and mercy. Such miracles happen every day. You can read about them in medical journals and hear of them in believing churches. In addition, we have been given many such examples throughout the Bible. One could argue, for example, that the Israelites were in slavery so that God's power would be shown through their deliverance. Word of that deliverance spread throughout the Middle East. The reason Rahab hid Joshua's two spies in Jericho was because she had heard of what their God had done to the Egyptians and to the Amorites (Josh. 2).

Truly, one could argue that a demonstration of God's power is the reason for each episode of suffering from which God saves someone. Yet, as we have seen, any one time of suffering could be for many different reasons. Because they suffered as they did, my friends are able to comfort others who are afflicted and are able to witness to others. And their own faith has been greatly strengthened.

We do not need to conjecture our way through the Bible to find episodes of suffering which glorified God. In two stories in the Book of John we are told specifically that that was why the person suffered. The lives described there are no less real than my friends' lives with whom this chapter began.

Imagine the parents in John 9. They probably did not believe her when the midwife first broke the news that their baby was blind. "See him turn his head to my voice?" the new mother probably cried.

"He would have been better off dead before he was born," the new father probably lamented, a lament he repeated through most of the boy's life. He knew his son would never run and play with the other boys and knew his son could never work at a trade with him. His son would be dependent all his life, for there was no occupation that did not require sight. The boy's mother would have wept and wailed and prayed and loved her little blind baby. Both probably asked often, "God, why? Why him? Why us?" The rabbis told them it must have been because of some sin committed by either of them or by one of their ancestors, though they knew of none.

As the boy grew, his mother taught him to do what chores he could. His father would have liked to take the boy to the synagogue. Because the blindness was thought to be punishment for somebody's sin, his son was not welcome there. So the father taught his boy at home.

With dread they faced the day when other boys went to be apprenticed and learn trades. With broken hearts, they gave their son a beggar's bowl, the only occupation fit for a blind boy.

Day after day he mumbled his thanks as people tossed in their shekels. Years passed and he grew to be a young man. His mother had long since ceased asking, "Why?" and had given up believing for the miracle that would give her son sight. This was just another day.

He was sitting there with his bowl, just like always, when he heard strangers stop and talk.

> "Rabbi, who sinned, this man or his parents, that he should be born blind?" Jesus answered, "It *was* neither *that* this man sinned, nor his parents; but *it was* so that the works of God might be displayed in him" (John 9:2-3).

All his life he had been told that his blindness was somebody's fault. After all, hadn't God told his ancestors that He would visit the sin of the fathers on the children to the third and fourth generations (Ex. 20:5)? He must be bearing the sins of somebody to have been born blind. Now here was a stranger they called "Rabbi" saying there was no sin, that he had been chosen by God to reveal God's power and goodness. He didn't feel chosen by God, suffering through the life he had, sitting there with a begging bowl.

Normally he didn't let anyone touch his eyes, although over the years many people had tried. But there was something about this stranger that made him want to sit still and let this man they called "Rabbi" spread on his eyes a paste He had made of spit and dirt. Perhaps it was because of what the Rabbi had said, that his blindness was not really a punishment.

Jesus said, "Go, wash in the pool of Siloam." And he made his way along the streets of Jerusalem to the ancient pool of water and washed the paste off his eyes.

His face dripped as he looked up from the water, and his life was transformed. "Oh, my God, so this is what your world looks like! I can't believe what you have done for me, Lord." He couldn't wait to get back to the corner to thank the stranger, but when he got there the stranger was gone.

What a hubbub ensued. No one could believe it. Even his neighbors and those who had known him as a beggar questioned if it was really he. Of course it was he. When he told them that he got his sight when he washed off the paste that the stranger had put on his eyes, the people dragged him to the Pharisees. They had known people who had lost their sight and had it restored, but no one who was born blind ever received sight as a grown man. How could the stranger do this? Hadn't the Pharisees said the man was born blind because of some sin? The people were confused.

Pharisees questioned him. When he said that the stranger must have been a prophet to have given him his sight, they didn't believe him and summoned the young man's parents. All his parents could do was say that it was, indeed, their son who had been born blind and now, obviously, he could see. They couldn't say what happened. They hadn't been there. Besides, they were afraid of the Pharisees, who had the power to keep them out of the synagogue for the rest of their lives.

The Pharisees told the man to give the glory to God, not the one who had healed him. The Pharisees would not admit that Jesus had been sent from God because He had healed on the Sabbath, breaking Pharisaical law. Jesus gave the man more than his sight. He gave him the courage to chastise the Pharisees. The man rebuked them with their own words:

> "Well, here is an amazing thing, that you do not know where He is from, and *yet* He opened my eyes. We know that God does not hear sinners; but if anyone is God-fearing and does His will, He hears him. Since the beginning of time it has never been heard that anyone opened the eyes of a person born blind. If this man were not from God, He could do nothing" (John 9:30-33).

The Pharisees put the young man out of the synagogue, but they could not refute the man's story. Everyone knew. Through Jesus curing that man's blindness many people came to faith.

It would be much easier if God told us just before our suffering began that our suffering was to be God's stage. It would be a comfort to know for certain that from this suffering others will come to faith by seeing God's power and mercy. It takes faith to trust that God is allowing our suffering to save others. We have opportunities to exercise our faith because God doesn't tell us as we suffer the reasons we are suffering. When we are in the midst of suffering, faith is all we have to hang onto; and often God's presence is very hard to find. The Bible shows us the way. Our second example is from John 11.

Having grown up in a Jewish home, I can imagine what life was like for Lazarus and his sisters Mary and Martha. We don't know when their parents died, but we know the girls had a brother to provide for them. Since they were not married, he had to be both brother and father to the two girls. In truth, they probably cared for each other. The girls would have taken care of the house. Perhaps Lazarus did not push them to marry. We know from Gospel references that they were a happy family, at least until Lazarus, a young man, got sick.

They were not too worried. After all, they were good friends of Jesus. They knew Jesus loved them and that He could perform miracles. All the women had to do was let Jesus know that his dear friend Lazarus was very sick.

So they sent a message. But Jesus didn't come. Quickly their brother's condition worsened. "Oh, Jesus, come! Don't let our brother die! You love him. We need him. You love us. Please," they probably prayed. Still He didn't come. The messenger might not have heard Jesus say, "This sickness is not to end in death, but for the glory of God, so that the Son of God may be glorified by it" (John 11:4).

Even if they had been told that Jesus said this, their faith might have been shaken. Jesus had said that the sickness was not to be unto death, but their beloved brother died. It couldn't be. Jesus wouldn't let it happen. But He did. Mary and Martha did not understand.

By Jewish law the body had to be cleansed, anointed, wrapped and entombed within 24 hours. They could not wait for Jesus to arrive. The whole village turned out to help and mourn with Mary and Martha. As per Jewish custom, the family stayed in the house, mourning. How they wept! Friends and neighbors brought food. They visited and reminisced and brought news of the outside world.

Someone rushed in with the news that Jesus was on the way. Too late. It was too late. Lazarus had been in the tomb for four days already. What could Jesus possibly say to comfort these women? Martha ran to meet Him.

"Lord, if You had been here, my brother would not have died. Even now I know that whatever You ask of God,

God will give You" (John 11:21-22).

She believed Jesus when he said, "I am the resurrection and the life; he who believes in Me will live even if he dies, and everyone who lives and believes in Me will never die" (John 11:25-26). But she thought He meant in the afterlife, during the final resurrection. Her brother had been dead for four days. What else could Jesus possibly mean?

When Jesus called for Mary, all the neighbors and friends who had been with her came too. They were desolate. Even those who believed in Him knew He came too late.

> Therefore, when Mary came where Jesus was, she saw Him, and fell at His feet, saying to Him, "Lord, if You had been here, my brother would not have died." When Jesus therefore saw her weeping, and the Jews who came with her also weeping, He was deeply moved in spirit and was troubled. . . . Jesus wept (John 11:32-33, 35).

God did not give my friend tumors. He did not make the baby blind in his mother's womb. He did not kill Lazarus. God does not cause or callously watch our suffering, waiting for just the right time to achieve maximum effect for His rescue. Whenever we suffer, God hears our groaning, as He did with the Israelites. He sees our tears, as He did Mary and Martha's. He hurts with us and He weeps. We are never alone in our suffering.

Jesus had the men move the stone from the entrance of the tomb and called Lazarus out. And out he came, still wrapped in his burial linens. Jesus had to tell the people to unwrap him. They were in shock. The Apostle John, who was there, comments,

> Therefore many of the Jews who came to Mary and saw what He had done, believed in Him (John 11:45).

What a testimony! Lazarus was not an obscure man in a distant, tiny village. He was a prominent man in Bethany, a town not far from Jerusalem. Word of his miracle spread. Multitudes came to faith because he had suffered and died early in life and then was raised from the dead.

> The large crowd of the Jews then learned that He was there; and they came, not for Jesus' sake only, but that they might also see Lazarus, whom He raised from the dead (John 12:9).

Whenever God relieves us of suffering through His power and mercy, others can be brought to faith. Remembering this will provide the blanket of peace my marine friend experienced, a backdrop of peace through which temporary explosions of anger, fear and frustration may emerge. Knowing others will be brought to faith will not remove the pain. My friend began our interview with the statement, "I wish God had chosen to do it differently. While clamps are on your head it's hard to see things God's way." He ended the interview, "I know the whole thing was part of God's plan. If anything had been different, it wouldn't have worked out."

Suffering is difficult, but often we just need to trust God and hang on. Only He knows the people who will be brought to faith in Jesus Christ by His work in your suffering.

Chapter 10

To Bring Others to Faith Through Our Testimony

Deuteronomy 28:10
So all the peoples of the earth shall see that you are called by the name of the Lord

Our courage and peace in the face of suffering gets people's attention. Witnessing our peace can bring others to faith.

How many hats do you wear? That is to say, how many groups do you represent? Our son represents boys his age and children who go to his school. As a Messianic Jew, he represents both Jews and Christians. He also represents Americans, people from our town and state, Tae Kwon Do black belts, kids in Little League, and our family. In other peoples' eyes we are all representatives of what group they see when they look at us.

The Southern Baptist Convention and Focus on the Family are two of the many groups who have called for their constituents to boycott the Disney Corporation and their products. They did this because the image the Disney name evokes to the world is no longer wholesome. When Walt Disney was alive, profits from Cinderella, Snow White, Mickey Mouse Club, and Disneyland went to give us Disney World with the Magic Kingdom, and Epcot Center that promoted international understanding. They were all creations of Walt Disney. The Disney name became synonymous with clean, wholesome family entertainment. After Walt Disney died, the Disney Corporation bought Miramar, and produced *Scream* and *Scream II*, realistic slasher horror movies in which teenagers kill people. They own the television network that produced *Ellen*, promoting homosexuality, and *Nothing Sacred*, attacking the Roman Catholic Church. For those of us who trusted the Disney name, it has been a betrayal.

Just as the Disney name used to mean something, being a child of God means something. When we are known as God's people but act in an ungodly manner, we betray all who believe that God's name stands for holiness. When people look at us they should see God, because in our behavior we represent Him. For those of us who are Christians and Jews, it is the most important hat we wear.

When you see children on a field trip who yell and push each other, who litter and take no regard of either their surroundings or the other people trying to enjoy them, what do you think? Most people think, "I'm glad my child doesn't go to that school," and, "I wonder what kind of families those children come from?" If the children are from a public school, you might think, "That is what public schools have come to." If they are from a Christian school, you might think, "Is that what Christian schools teach?" Or, if you were not a believer, you might think that is what Christian children are like. If the field trip took the children to a distant city, state, or country, the people who witnessed the behavior would also ascribe the behavior to the town from which the children came, or the state, or even the United States.

Americans have a terrible image abroad in some places, an image that is, unfortunately, sometimes well deserved. I was once in Stratford, England, Shakespeare's home. It is a quiet little village marked by cottages made of waddle and daub, a construction that looks much like whitewashed stucco. The streets were narrow, and flowers bloomed in neat beds everywhere. The panorama created an aura of tranquillity unbroken even by the many tourists. Peace pervaded the scene of white cottages, green grass, wisps of white clouds streaking across blue skies, and sprinkles of white, yellow and red flowers.

It was a Sunday. We went into the local church, the only place, ironically enough, we could change dollars for pounds on a Sunday. I don't know which came first, the serenity of the town or the tranquillity of the church, but God's peace filled His sanctuary. As we entered, we saw notices posted asking that no flash pictures be taken and that people speak quietly, so we tourists wouldn't disturb any who were there to worship.

The atmosphere drew me in. As I slid into an empty pew about half way toward the beautifully carved but simple altar, I was grateful for the dim lighting and the people speaking in hushed voices. I felt God's presence and wanted to pray.

Suddenly the peace was shattered by a booming Texas drawl, "Waahl, ha'ell, if I want to take pictures, ain't nobody gonna stop me!" And pop, pop, pop exploded the flash of the camera.

I felt both assaulted and ashamed. I was ashamed that he was American and that Texas was part of the union. He made me sick with the same sickness I know whenever someone from one of the groups of which I am a part gets publicity for ungodly behavior. The most painful for me is when someone Jewish or Christian brings shame on God's name. For all who call ourselves either Christian or Jew, we are representatives of God in everything we do.

The more fame we achieve, the greater our responsibility to reflect God so others may be drawn to Him. To do otherwise will cause others to blame God for our behavior and will turn people away from God. David was called into account when he set up Uriah to be killed in battle so he could marry Uriah's wife, Bathsheba. God revealed David's sins and punishment to Nathan, the prophet.

Because David's sins were so egregious and would cause people to turn away from God, the child that David and Bathsheba had conceived in adultery would not long live.

Nathan told David,

> "The Lord has taken away your sin; you shall not die. However, because by this deed you have given occasion to the enemies of the Lord to blaspheme, the child also that is born to you shall surely die" (2 Sam. 12:13b-14).

This was not a punishment to their baby. Infants that die are taken immediately to God's glorious heaven. But it was a punishment to David and Bathsheba.

Like David, when we sin, we cause others to think, "So, that's what his God condones," or, "So that is what Christians are like." They blaspheme God because of our behavior.

Over the centuries, Satan has gotten people to do unspeakable things in Jesus' name. The Crusades, the Inquisition, the wars between Catholics and Protestants in earlier centuries in Europe and England, and today in Northern Ireland; the war in Bosnia between Serbians and Croatians—all are prime examples of those who claim to *be* Christians not living *as* Christians. Some of the tyrants in western civilization have hidden behind Jesus' name. My husband was a born again believer when we first started keeping company. The first time he approached me about Jesus, I blurted out, "Do you know how many of my people your people killed in the name of your God? What on earth would I want with your God?!" Christianity meant killing to me because history books are filled with political wars in the name of Christianity.

When people who call themselves Christian, like the Serbian Christians in Bosnia and the Catholics and Protestants in Northern Ireland, do terrible things, it causes people to turn away from God, to blaspheme.

A man blew up an abortion clinic, killing several people. He was on national news when he declared he did it for Jesus, that God had told him to wipe out the evil of abortion. No one knows how many nonbelievers thought that Christianity teaches followers to kill people who break God's law. Only God knows how many were turned away from Him by that man.

Scripture admonishes us again and again to live godly lives as His representatives. Peter wrote,

> Make sure that none of you suffer as a murderer, or thief, or evildoer, or a troublesome meddler; but if *anyone suffers* as a Christian, he is not to be ashamed, but is to glorify God in this name [Christ] (1 Pet. 4:15-16).

Even in our suffering, God is to be glorified. Peter wrote these words to us, who are "born again to a living hope through the resurrection of Jesus Christ from the dead" (1 Pet. 1:3b). The citizens of this world are murderers, thieves, evildoers and meddlers. They are marked by wickedness, greed, envy, strife, deceit, and malice (Rom. 1:29). We are not to look like them, behave like them, or think like them. We are to be aliens and not of the world.

> For all that is in the world, the lust of the flesh and the lust of the eyes and the boastful pride of life, is not from

the Father, but is from the world. The world is passing away, and also its lusts; but the one who does the will of God lives forever (1 John 2:16-17).

We will be aliens on earth if we try to lead godly lives, for we do not live in a godly world. Our home is in heaven.

Yet, there is more to being a representative of God than staying out of trouble. We are to be positive representatives so others will see God when they see the fruit of the Spirit in us (Gal. 5:22). Because of our obedience to God and the blessings that come with that closeness, others will take notice. That is the way it should be. As God told the Israelites,

> "The Lord will establish you as a holy people to Himself, as He swore to you, if you keep the commandments of the Lord your God and walk in His ways. *So all the peoples of the earth shall see that you are called by the name of the Lord* (italics mine); and they will be afraid of you" (Deut. 28:9-10).

It is the same promise for us. If we walk in God's ways, the world will see that we belong to God. People fear what is different and we will be different. The difference will not be in material blessings, for the gospel is preached to the poor as well as the wealthy. The difference will not be in our having lives without conflict or pain. For the Lord said,

> Blessed are you when people insult you and persecute you, and falsely say all kinds of evil against you because of Me. Rejoice and be glad, for your reward in heaven is great; for in the same way they persecuted the prophets who were before you (Matt. 5:11-12).

To Bring Others to Faith Through Our Testimony

The Lord does not say, "Blessed are you *if* people insult you." He says, "*when* people insult you...." We who belong to God are to be different not only in our godly conduct, but also in our response to the trials that come into our lives. When people mistreat us, we are to rejoice and be glad. When the world sees that difference, they will take note, and many will come to faith. One reason God will allow us to suffer is to show nonbelievers the difference faith makes in the face of suffering. He first allowed Satan to afflict Job to show Satan how a righteous man suffers.

> There was a man in the land of Uz whose name was Job; and that man was blameless, upright, fearing God and turning away from evil. Seven sons and three daughters were born to him. His possessions also were 7,000 sheep, 3,000 camels, 500 yoke of oxen, 500 female donkeys, and very many servants; and that man was the greatest of all the men of the east (Job 1: 1-3).

Job was a success by every measurement. His sons and daughters held feasts for each other. He had enormous wealth. He was humble before God, making sacrifices on behalf of his children in case, during their feasting, his children sinned and cursed God in their hearts (Job 1:4-5). Job was one of God's children and God had greatly blessed him.

Although few of us have Job's riches, God has blessed us in many ways. A popular song from my childhood told of counting blessings instead of sheep. When, upon occasion, I awake during the night and have trouble falling back asleep, I follow that advice. I never run out of blessings to count: our faith, our lives, our health, each other, our children, people in our lives, our home, our country, etc. For each of us our lists of blessings are, literally, endless.

But it is not that we are blessed with family and friends and material possessions that others notice the difference between the world and us. The difference is most apparent by our reactions to suffering. And God might allow us to suffer so that others will see that difference, as He did with Job.

> Now there was a day when the sons of God came to present themselves before the Lord, and Satan also came among them. The Lord said to Satan, "From where do you come?" Then Satan answered the Lord and said, "From roaming about on the earth and walking around on it." And the Lord said to Satan, "Have you considered My servant Job? For there is no one like him on the earth, a blameless and upright man, fearing God and turning away from evil" (Job 1:6-8).

In the following verses, Satan challenges God, saying that Job is righteous because God has blessed and protected Him. Satan thinks if God removes His hedge, i.e., His protection, from Job, Job will curse God. So God gives Satan permission to afflict Job to show Satan the difference between the way someone who belongs to God accepts suffering and the way people who don't belong to God suffer.

Just as God works through people to bring about good in the world, so Satan often works through people to bring about suffering. The Sabeans steal all Job's oxen and donkeys and kill all the servants attending the livestock. The Chaldeans steal all Job's camels and kill those servants. Fire destroys all Job's sheep and the servants with them, and strong winds collapse Job's oldest son's house where all Job's children had gathered, killing all of them (Job 1:13-19).

Let's think about what Job's been through. Working and getting laid off is scary. Losing a business is devastating, even if the failure is over a long period of time. Through no fault of his own, Job lost all of his wealth and all of his means for rebuilding his wealth in just a day. Job lost all of his ten children, children who would give him grandchildren, children who would run his business and take care of him when he got old, children whom he loved. Losing a child is the greatest loss a person can endure. Yet he did not curse God or even blame Him (Job 1:22).

We all know people of the world who curse God routinely. If they drop something, or get a red light when they are in a hurry, or misplace something, they curse God. They do it without thinking. Most give no thought to God. Cursing is just an automatic reaction to being annoyed. Contrast that reaction to Job's, who had just lost everything.

> Then Job arose and tore his robe and shaved his head, and he fell to the ground and worshiped. He said,
> "Naked I came from my mother's womb,
> And naked I shall return there.
> The Lord gave and the Lord has taken away.
> Blessed be the name of the Lord" (Job 1:20-21).

It is all too much for Job's wife. She, too, has lost all her wealth, all her children and, now, even her husband's health. She tells Job to curse God and die (Job 2: 9). He has gone from a man with everything to a man with nothing, not his health, his wealth, or his children. His response to her was: "Shall we indeed accept good from God and not accept adversity?" (Job 2:10).

That response can only be made or understood by a person who believes. The world will tell us to curse God, as Job's wife did. Some will mock us and lie about us for not cursing God. Peter warned us of this.

Keep a good conscience so that in the thing in which you are slandered, those who revile your good behavior in Christ will be put to shame. For it is better, if God should will it so, that you suffer for doing what is right rather than for doing what is wrong (1 Pet. 3:16-17).

People of faith are to be windows through which others see God. Some, like those Peter and Jesus warned us about, will ridicule and persecute us. But some will see God's peace and strength in our suffering. They will want to know the source of our strength and come to faith. Whether the people are mocking you, attacking you, or curious about why you are different, be ready to talk to them. Peter tells us always to be ready to explain to everyone who asks us "to give an account for the hope that is in you, yet with gentleness and reverence" (1 Pet. 3:15). By telling us to be ready, Peter does not mean to prepare and rehearse what we will say. He means to allow ourselves to be used by God to reach people whenever they ask or challenge us. Be available. We need not prepare. Indeed, Jesus told us not to prepare:

> "So make up your minds not to prepare beforehand to defend yourselves; for I will give you utterance and wisdom which none of your opponents will be able to resist or refute" (Luke 21:14-15).

The Holy Spirit will give you the words (Mark 13:11). He always gives me the words I need to share my faith. Time and again I have been in situations like the ones I found myself in recently on a series of plane trips. It was a long trip that entailed five different flights and waiting times in several airports. As a Jewish believer, I wear both a cross and a Star of David. People I sat near saw the cross and star, or they saw

To Bring Others to Faith Through Our Testimony

me writing and wanted to know who I was, why I wore both the cross and star, and/or what my book was about. When I replied, the people started talking. Some were hungry to hear what God has said about suffering, especially their suffering. Some were anxious to challenge me. All demanded an answer. I was taken by complete surprise, although these encounters happen to me often. There is no way to prepare for such encounters. The Holy Spirit has never failed to give me words the people questioning me needed to hear.

Often we don't even need words. People can see the difference. When we are calm when those of the world panic, when we are at peace when those of the world are worried or angry, others see the difference. Some will be brought to faith.

That is what happened at Jesus' crucifixion. Two criminals also were being crucified, one on either side of Jesus. One of the criminals mocked Jesus, even as there will be those who will mock us for holding onto our faith as we suffer. One of the criminals was brought to faith. He told the other criminal he should fear God, since they were being condemned, and because Jesus didn't deserve to die. Then he asked Jesus to remember him when Jesus came into His kingdom (Luke 23:39-43).

How did the criminal know that Jesus had done nothing wrong and was a man of God? It was not by Jesus' preaching or teaching. It was not because of great miracles he had seen Jesus perform. While Jesus was dying on the cross, he might have heard Jesus say, "Father, forgive them; for they do not know what they are doing" (Luke 23:34). Or he could have noticed Jesus' peace and inner strength as He was being led to Golgotha and tied and nailed to the cross.

Job's response was not of this world. Our response does not have to be of this world. In Ecclesiastes, God told us that we would have hard times in our lives. God strengthens us and gives us peace during these hard times. We need only trust him.

God *did* restore Job's life and fortunes (Job 42:10-17).

Like each of us, David experienced hard times, but he knew his source of strength. His song can be our song. He wrote these words when the Philistines seized him in Gath:

> You have taken account of my wanderings;
> Put my tears in Your bottle;
> Are *they* not in Your book?
> Then my enemies will turn back in the day when I call;
> This I know, that God is for me.
> In God, *whose* word I praise,
> In the Lord, *whose* word I praise,
> In God I have put my trust, I shall not be afraid.
> What can man do to me? (Ps. 56:8-11).

God counts our tears. He weeps with us, as Jesus wept with Mary and Martha. When you are faced with your suffering, repeat David's words, "In God I have put my trust, I shall not be afraid."

When He allows us to suffer, there is always a reason, sometimes several. My friend with the brain tumor understands this. He and his wife know that those who witnessed the miracle of his healing might come to faith because of what they saw. They also know that, coming through that terrible ordeal, they must minister to others who have physical afflictions. They know their faith has been strengthened. And their story is here because they also know that through their testimony of God's peace and power, others will be brought to faith.

What is your testimony? It need not be so dramatic as the stories here. Thankfully, few of us suffer as Job or Jesus or my friend. Still, God delivers us in less dramatic ways that provide testimony to His power and mercy, testimony that can bring others to faith. For example, many times I have had the opportunity to tell people of how God provided for us miraculously when my husband lost his job at age 57, with five children, two of whom were in college.

When the company he had worked for closed, almost everyone lost his job. It was a time of downsizing throughout the aerospace and defense industries. With all the professional people on the market at once, new jobs were scarce. The engineers and managers went through outplacement services together. They wrote resumes and learned job search techniques. Many were panicked and marveled at my husband's peace. He told them, "You might have gotten laid off, but I didn't. I work for the Lord. He has a job transfer for me. I don't know where I'm being transferred to yet, but He does. He's in control, so I'm not worried. I trust Him."

On two occasions, days before the mortgage payment was due, he got a call from some company wanting him to do just enough consulting to pay the bills. The world calls it coincidence. They will always call it coincidence. We knew it was God.

In Matthew's Gospel there's the story of Jesus providing a coin to pay the temple taxes for Himself and Peter. The Lord told him to go fishing—in other words, to do what he knew he was supposed to do. When Peter did and pulled up a fish, just the right coin was in its mouth to pay their taxes (Matt. 17:24-27). Like Peter, my husband turned to God, then continued to do what he knew he should—make looking for a job a full time job. God provided for us, just like He did for Peter.

Still, a career position did not emerge right away. Our prayers had begun, "God, find us a job here. We have our home and friends and family and a daughter in college here."

Why God Lets People Suffer

When we changed our prayer to "God, we want only to serve you. Send us where You need us," so many job offers came in we had to ask God to sort them out for us.

The world can be a dark and hopeless place. But God is a miracle-working God, and stories of miracles give people hope. That is why Jesus told us that we are the light of the world (Matt. 5:14). Our testimony is our light. We can't hide it under a bushel. If people see God through our words and through our behavior, our testimony can bring others to faith, testimony we would not have if we never had to experience suffering.

Chapter 11

To Contrast This Life to Eternity

Romans 8:18
For I consider that the sufferings of this present time are not worthy to be compared with the glory that is to be revealed to us

This chapter could have been subtitled "What a Difference Heaven Makes." It makes all the difference in the world. Belief in heaven changes our view of dying, and it also changes how we live our lives and how we feel about suffering.

Our son's grandparents call themselves "cultural" Jews. They go to synagogue, try to be good, kind people, and feel virtuous. They pick and choose from the Bible as to what they believe. It is what Isaiah warns us of: "Woe to those who are wise in their own eyes, and clever in their own sight!" (Is. 5:21). They grew up in families that went to synagogue but never talked about the reality of God or His presence in their lives. Neither did they view the Hebrew Bible (our Old Testament) as God's Word. They are just like many people who call themselves Christian today. Their stands on such things as homosexuality and abortion are not Scriptural. Neither is their understanding of salvation.

I once asked Grandpa, who values only the culture of his religion, about his spirit or soul. He replied, "I don't think people have souls. When I die, I'll become worm food. That's all." He is not unusual. It is a common belief in our society.

Many Jews have chosen not to believe their own Scriptures, where we are told that we have souls and that when we die our souls depart from us. Rachel died as her son, Benjamin, was born.

> It came about as her soul was departing (for she died), that she named him Ben-oni; but his father called him Benjamin (Gen. 35:18).

These people can often recite the great commandment, to love God with all their hearts, and with all their *souls*, and with all their strength (Deut. 6:5, Mark 12:30). Yet, they have chosen not to believe that they have souls. They prefer to look at death as Hamlet longed to:

> To die: to sleep; No more; and by a sleep to say we end the heartache and the thousand natural shocks the flesh is heir to. 'Tis a consummation highly to be wished. To die; to sleep... (W. Shakespeare, Hamlet, Act 3, Scene 1).

Hamlet continues to say that thoughts of what will happen to our souls after we die keeps us from committing suicide. So the quoted portion is not the position where Hamlet ends, but it is the position of cultural Jews. Like all of us, heartache and a thousand natural shocks have marked their lives. Death, they hope, is an end to suffering. Yet, like the Israelites who wanted to turn back to slavery (Ex. 14:10-12), they will cling to this life of suffering because that is all they know and all they have chosen to believe.

Since they do not believe they have souls, they certainly do not believe Daniel's prophecy:

> Many of those who sleep in the dust of the ground will

To Contrast This Life to Eternity

awake, these to everlasting life, but the others to disgrace *and* everlasting contempt (Dan. 12:2).

Or Jesus' words,

"And these will go away into eternal punishment, but the righteous into eternal life" (Matt. 25:46).

I understand their choosing not to believe. They do not believe, they say, because there is no concrete proof of life after death. They say they know no one who has come back from the dead to tell them about it. Believers know Jesus came back, but nonbelievers can't accept Jesus' resurrection.

There are also, however, innumerable accounts of people who were pronounced dead and then came back to life. Their descriptions are nearly identical: a bright light that gets ever closer, until they are pulled or sent back to this world; and a sense of well being which they did not want to leave. Nonbelievers cannot explain the phenomenon. They say those persons could not have really been dead and that being so close to death might produce a common delusion. If they discard Jesus and all the testimonies of people who have died and come back, it is true that they have no concrete proof of life after death.

It reminds me of the story of Lazarus that Jesus told (Luke 16:19-31). Lazarus was a sick beggar, whose name means "God is my help." There was a rich man who refused to help the beggar. When they both died, the beggar went to heaven and the rich man went to hell. When the rich man cried out to Abraham far away in heaven to let Lazarus go back to his house to warn the rich man's family, Abraham replied, "If they do not listen to Moses and the Prophets, they will not be persuaded even if someone rises from the dead" (16:31).

People have come back from the dead, and still there are those who do not believe.

Besides, it is dangerous to believe the Scriptures, for the Scriptures say that we have souls, that those souls depart from us when we die, and that our souls will be judged. There is the problem. These people do not want to consider the possibility of everlasting contempt or punishment. It is easier to think all their suffering will be over when they die than to think that they will be judged. Unfortunately for them, their choice not to believe does not change the truth of the Scriptures. Truth is not dependent on whether anyone believes it. And the truth is that we have souls and that after we die our souls will stand for judgment, either covered by the righteousness of Jesus (1 Thess. 5:9), or laden with our own sin (John 8:24).

Why do so many people reject God's salvation? If they read the Bible they would know that Jesus fulfilled all of the prophecies of His birth (Micah 5:2), His purpose (Is. 61:1-3), and His death (Ps. 22:1-18, Is. 53). One stumbling block, if they do read the Bible, is that there is no clear promise of universal eternal life and no clear description of either heaven or hell in the Old Testament, although there is a description of heavenly hosts standing by God (1 Kg. 22:19); and a description of the train of God's robe filling the temple where the Seraphim with six wings are praising God (Is. 6:1-3).

My son has a jigsaw puzzle of a jungle scene. When the puzzle is all assembled, if he looks very carefully, he can find ten animals camouflaged and carefully hidden among the branches and undergrowth. They are there, but unless one knows what to look for, one could easily not even know that they are there. It is that way with the concepts of heaven and hell in the Old Testament.

While the Old Testament lays the groundwork for the

To Contrast This Life to Eternity

New, it clearly focuses on this life. God promises blessings on the Israelite people for their obedience to the commandments He has given them. Deuteronomy 28:2-14 speaks of blessings of land and livestock, prosperity, rain, children, protection against their enemies, and corporate blessings as a nation. All of those blessings have to do with this life. Not one blessing mentions eternal life.

Likewise, Deuteronomy 27:14-26 and 28:15-68 outline God's promises of curses on those who do not obey Him and instead worship false gods. The curses are all related to this life. They talk of sickness and fear, of desolation, famine and conflict. The curses do not include eternal punishment.

The New Testament changes our focus. Clearly, Jesus did not want our lives to be spent solely on this life. He told us this many times. Nor are we to waste our energies worrying about this life. The focus of God's kingdom and eternal life in heaven frees us from that:

> "For this reason I say to you, do not worry about *your* life, as *to* what you will eat; nor for your body, as *to* what you will put on. For life is more than food, and the body than clothing. Consider the ravens, for they neither sow nor reap; and they have no storeroom nor barn; and yet God feeds them; how much more valuable you are than the birds! And do not seek what you shall eat, and what you shall drink, and do not keep worrying. For all these things the nations of the world eagerly seek; but your Father knows that you need these things. But seek for His kingdom, and these things shall be added to you" (Luke 12:22-24, 29-31).

Jesus did not talk about full barns or lives free of diseases. Rather, He told us to seek God and trust Him. We are to consider the ravens. Ravens are scavengers. All that they have, God has given them. All that we have, God has given us. Oh, yes, the ravens must fly about looking for food, and we, too, must work. Jesus wants us to recognize what God pointed out in Deuteronomy, that if it rains, it is God's gift. He wants us to realize that the jobs we have He has given us, and He has given us the ability to do them. He takes care of us, just as He takes care of the ravens. We must be like Moses, do our best and leave the rest to God.

We would all like full barns. Ravens, probably, would like to find their food right beside them, so they wouldn't have to search for it, and, perhaps, have birdhouses so that the rain wouldn't fall on them. God does not provide ravens with birdhouses. He provides them and us with what we need.

Most of us have trouble distinguishing between want and need. I know families that think they need a television for each person in the family. I know couples who both work, despite having young children, because they think they need to belong to a health club and drive late model cars or live in exclusive neighborhoods. Children are notorious for confusing want and need. "I *need* that toy." "I *need* my own phone." In love, God will straighten out His children who are confused between want and need.

I have a dear friend who is a single mom. In the midst of her suffering she praises God. She had a nice house, drove a nice car, lived what the world calls a good life and she did it on her own, she thought. Even without a college degree, she had a very responsible, well-paid position. Over just a few months, God allowed her life to be stripped of everything but her daughter and His love.

First and foremost, she was stripped of her belief in the false gods of money, position, and possessions. Many of us trust those same false gods. Our sense of security comes from what we have achieved or what we have attained. It is a false security because all we have comes from God. As Job said, "The Lord gave and the Lord has taken away" (Job 1:21). She says He stripped her of another false god, the belief in the god of freedom. She thought she was free to impulsively live as she pleased. She had to learn that none of us is free. Oh, yes, we live in the land of freedom and permissiveness in America, but freedom is only an illusion. As Jesus said, "Truly, truly, I say to you, everyone who commits sin is the slave of sin" (John 8:34). And as Paul said,

> Thanks be to God that though you were slaves of sin, you became obedient from the heart to that form of teaching to which you were committed, and having been freed from sin, you became slaves of righteousness (Rom. 6:17-18).

My friend had never learned that the drive to pursue ungodly things is bondage, or that God's power to free us from those bonds frees us to serve Him. It is an either/or choice. You either choose to be a slave to sin or choose to be God's servant. Faith in the security of our own personal freedom was, to my friend, the most important god that God destroyed.

God has provided for my friend and her daughter's needs day by day.

When my friend's daughter was going blind and she could not afford the contact lenses that could retard the progression of her blindness, God provided the lenses through the Lions Club, a friend who split the cost, and a doctor who made no profit, though he certainly could have. My friend depends on God and thanks Him for everything. She has learned she can trust the Lord. Knowing God will provide and that Jesus is even now preparing a room for her in heaven (John 14:2), she is at peace.

The point is that God will provide in this life. We are not to worry about it or even focus on it. Jesus admonishes us,

> "Do not store up for yourselves treasures on earth, where moth and rust destroy, and where thieves break in and steal. But store up for yourselves treasures in heaven, where neither moth nor rust destroys, and where thieves do not break in or steal; for where your treasure is, there your heart will be also" (Matt. 6:19-21).

What a difference the change of focus makes. When we see that our span of life on earth is so short compared to eternity, we start to see God's perspective. God does not want us to miss the big picture. If we focus on our own situation, we lose sight of the big picture.

Hurricane Andrew was financially the most devastating hurricane this country has ever suffered. Photos of the damage show mile after mile of buildings laid waste all across southern Florida. My brother, who has Lou Gehrig's disease, lives in Miami where hurricane Andrew hit land. The hurricane passed through their neighborhood, and we witnessed another miracle.

My brother and sister-in-law live on what is nearly an estate. They have a beautiful two-story house with a pool under a screened enclosure to keep out the bugs when they are sitting out or swimming. The trees around three sides of the house are old and stately, providing charm and shade. In back are towering, prolific grapefruit and avocado trees. The tennis court was surrounded on three sides by nearly two hundred pine trees.

When the call came to evacuate, my brother and his family escaped farther north and inland. After the storms they drove home not knowing what they would face. They passed mile after mile of flattened buildings, of cars and boats that had been flung through the air to land haphazardly. The destruction was horrific on their street. Trees had fallen on houses, crashing through roofs, tearing out walls. Then they saw their home. They couldn't believe it; we couldn't believe it. The pine trees were all down, scattered about like a dropped box of matchsticks. They tore through the fences and tore up the tennis court. The tennis court and the ground around it looked as if a bomb had been dropped. But their house was safe. The only damage to the house was caused by one tree that had ripped through the screened enclosure over the pool and had pulled away a small section of roof as it fell. It was a miracle.

When they looked at the devastation to their backyard, their hearts sank. Yet, surrounded by the devastation of their neighbors who had lost large portions of their houses, my brother and his family realized what they were suffering was nothing in comparison. When we look at nothing more than our tiny piece of fortune, or our suffering, we miss the big picture.

If we hike in the mountains or along a quiet beach and only look at the ground and our feet when we walk, we miss God's majesty. While visions of mountains or endless prairies or oceans are awesome and hint at God's power and glory, they are nothing compared to the view we have been given of heaven, a heaven that has been promised to us.

> For I consider that the sufferings of this present time are not worthy to be compared with the glory that is to be revealed to us (Rom. 8:18).

Knowing heaven is waiting makes all the difference in

facing death. To those who do not believe that the Bible is truth, death is the end, not the beginning of eternity with God. People who believe that they have no souls and that death is the end see no need for a savior. This life is all they have. To them the suffering in this life is pointless. They will fight it to their last breath and will curse the day they or someone they love dies.

I have a friend who is afraid to die. She knows how she has sinned in her life and she has not forgiven herself for those sins. Most of the time she knows that Jesus died for all of our sins, and that our sins were paid for, covered and forgiven by His blood. But there are times she feels so guilt ridden and unworthy that she can't believe He would die for *her*. That is why she is afraid to die. She knows God's word, but does not trust it. Although she has seen God keep His promises throughout her life, she must be reassured that He will keep His promise of eternal life. Without the trust in God's promise of heaven, there is no peace in our lives.

Knowing heaven is waiting makes all the difference in facing death. Nothing can show this difference better than this true story of the death of a child from cancer. I do not use the family's name because they want to draw attention to God's love, not to themselves.

This friend had endometriosis and had been told that they could not have children. So she knows her son was truly a gift from God, a miracle child, born into their baseball family. My friend's father had been a professional baseball player. Her husband is head coach of baseball at a large university and has been an Olympic baseball coach. Their son was growing up a chip off the old block. Baseball was in his blood. He loved it, but he loved God more.

Even before he got sick, everyone knew he was close to God. Children and adults alike were drawn to him. He

To Contrast This Life to Eternity

showed his faith in the little ways that make up everyday life, like making a point to treat a younger child nicely when the older kids around him were making fun of him. After he was sick, he often encouraged adults to accept the challenges God had put before them, as he did, with faith and love. He did not complain, and he was not afraid.

The routines and rituals of the Catholic faith were a part of him, and he never made any effort to hide it. Frequently, on Sunday nights as a teenager having fun with his friends 20 minutes away from church, he'd announce he had to go so he wouldn't be late for the special mass for teenagers. Rather than give him grief about splitting up the fun, some of the friends stopped what they were doing and went with him. Throughout his life, just because the way he was, he kept bringing people to God. He was a special child.

It was nearly a year from the time he was diagnosed with Ewing's carcinoma until the Lord took him. His father is a national figure in baseball. During that year people all over the country prayed continuously for his son's healing, but that was not God's plan. We were all thinking of the life he would miss, of the contribution he would make, and of the joy he was to his family. We hurt for his parents and his extended family. We were all saying, "Our will, not Thy will be done." All of us—except him.

During the last month of his life on earth perhaps a hundred people came to see him, mostly other children. He was hooked up to IVs and plugged into oxygen tubes. The chemotherapy had left him bald. They came to see his electric smile and dancing eyes. They came to say good-bye and mourn, but they got joy and hope instead. He knew he was going to heaven and he was not afraid. He knew he would soon see Jesus and Mary and his Father. He loved to share the joy he had, even with the pain and the tubes and certain death.

The friends had known him mostly through baseball, so they all understood his baseball imagery. They had all played or watched games that were close when the opposing team hit the ball. They had all at sometime watched the flight of the ball and pictured themselves making the winning play when the ball took a bad hop, bouncing the opposite direction from what they had expected. They all knew what it was like to deal with those unexpected bad hops, and they all knew life was like that, full of unexpected bad hops.

I suspect you know what it is like too. Your life is going along smoothly when something comes out of the blue. Wham! You hardly know what hit you. Maybe it's a car accident, or a job lay off, or a loved one getting seriously ill, or your spouse saying he/she wants a divorce, or your teenager telling you she's pregnant. Perhaps it is something small, like your babysitter quitting, leaving you with a job and no child care, or your car suddenly needing expensive repairs, or a promotion you counted on going to someone else. Those are the bad hops, the unexpected and painful turns in our lives.

When his friends came over to try to cheer him up and to mourn, he comforted them. With sparkling eyes, he flashed them his dazzling smile and laughed, "Guys, Guys, where I'm going there are no bad hops!"

Perhaps the greatest sorrow is that of a parent who has lost a child. I remember my father repeatedly saying that his one hope was that his children would bury him, that he would never have to bury one of his children. How could my friend accept God's taking the only child she could ever have? He was only 16. This was a child not only special to she and her husband and their extended family; he was special to the whole community.

Yet, when I talked to my friend, she did not talk about her

loss. She talked about where her son was and his getting there. She shared favorite Scripture verses and absolutely glowed with the love of God. She pointed out that the base where the batter starts and runs are scored is not called first base. First base is the first base the runners run to. Neither is it called fourth base, although it is where the runners go after passing third base. It is called "Home." She mused, "It is like heaven. We start there and the goal of every baseball player is to cross home plate, to get back home. My son hit a home run. He's run all the bases and he is home. He is in heaven."

She reaches through the pages of this book to warn us not to be too absorbed in our own existence, because when we are so absorbed it is easy to forget that this life is just a beginning. She warns that it is easy to get lulled into seeing life and death through the world's eyes. The world says their son is dead, but she knows differently. She said, "Jesus didn't promise us eternal death, but eternal life. He went to heaven to prepare rooms for us, even for my son. Our son did not die, he went to heaven. And heaven is perfect. There are no tears or sadness or pain in heaven."

The world says God deserted my friend. It says He didn't answer her fervent prayers. Yet, my friend is comforted by God, who watched His own Son die. She knows He loved Jesus as much as she and her husband loved their son. She knows He knows how she feels and she looks to Jesus for the courage in all things to say to our Father, "Your will be done" (Matt. 26:42).

The world says that God should not have taken her son away, that death is the end, the ultimate punishment. Christians know that it is the beginning of an eternity with God. When she thinks about never being a grandmother or the events she would be a part of in her son's life had he not gone to heaven, she realizes she is thinking of herself. How could a mother who really loved her child want that child to endure all the suffering that is part of this life rather than be in heaven? She misses their son very much, but she has peace and a joy that only comes with faith.

She knows that God has a purpose for each of us (Prov. 16:4). Once when she was praying, she felt a supernatural peace and the sense that her son had a purpose on earth, that he had finished his work, and that God had taken him home. A priest agreed with her and told her that her son had touched more lives in 16 years than most of us will if we live to be 90.

Her joy and inspiration are infectious. She has that peace that surpasses understanding. More than that, she has a faith and trust and love of God that can only be the Holy Spirit shining through.

The final point is that heaven is more than a better place, it is perfect. My friend recognizes that this life is not always so great. People are hurting physically, mentally, emotionally, and spiritually. There is sickness and anger and fear. There is divorce and abortion and hunger and war. Yet people cling to life, as if there were nothing better.

For the most part, people don't like change. The Israelites complained that they should have stayed back in Egypt as slaves. They no more believed in a Promised Land than modern skeptics believe in heaven. How bad did it have to be to get the Israelites to leave Egypt? How bad does it have to be for us to stop looking at this life as if losing it were a punishment?

The suffering in this life makes more real the life we have waiting for us in heaven. Heaven is the hook we can hang onto. As Paul wrote to Timothy, "The Lord will rescue me from every evil deed, and will bring me safely to His heavenly kingdom" (2 Timothy 4:18).

To Contrast This Life to Eternity

Heaven is the goal, the reward we can count on, the promise of an ending that is really but a beginning. Remember my friend's admonition, not to get mired in the world. For we are not of the world—we belong to God (Lev. 20:26, John 15:19). God will sustain us in this life while we fulfill His purpose for our lives. Then He will bring us home.

Chapter 12

From Faith to Trust to Joy

Psalm 56:3
When I am afraid, I will trust in You

How do we know someone loves us? There is no proof enough for the person unwilling to believe and trust. When a child has faith that his parents love him, he accepts their discipline and advice because his faith has led him to trust their concern for his welfare. Faith leads to trust. We can experience joy in our suffering only when we trust God and His Word. His Word tells us that He loves us so much that He gave us His only Son, that whoever believes in Him will have everlasting life (John 3:16). That kind of faith will lead us to joy in suffering.

To live without faith and trust is lonely and frightening. To trust in the wrong people can be fatal. Some people still put their faith in our government. Once upon a time, not that very long ago, most Americans had faith in our government and our leaders. Then we had President Nixon, who was forced to resign, and President Clinton, who brought us the worst sex scandal in our history. Now special prosecutors abound and faith in the government is hard to come by.

Faith in science is easier for many Americans. I know people who would like to change the motto on our coins from "In God We Trust" to "In Science We Trust." My brother with

Lou Gehrig's disease once had faith in himself. When he found he could not overcome the disease by the effort of his will, he turned his faith to science. Now he sits and heroically declares that he will not die until after scientists have discovered a cure. Despite a life of total disability and dependence, he will fight for his life with every ounce of his emaciated body. Death will not be a welcome home. He does not believe that the Bible is God's Word.

He has this faith in science because discoveries in medicines, equipment, and procedures over the last fifty years have exceeded most people's imaginations. Yet, God tells us, "Trust in the Lord with all your heart and do not lean on your own understanding" (Prov. 3:5). Ultimate faith in science is foolish. Nearly every month there is a discovery that throws out previously esteemed medical and scientific theories. Most recently astronomers on Mt. Hopkins discovered evidence of new solar systems, which, if true, would make obsolete the previously held scientific theories of planet formation and formation of the universe. And, despite everything science can do, our bodies still age, deteriorate, and die. Only God can give us eternal life.

But it does not have to be either God or science in which we believe. I have a friend who is a world-renowned scientist and a devout Christian. Instead of being elevated by his own importance, he is humbled. He is an astrophysicist who holds prayer services in his office every morning for any students or faculty who care to attend. He understands that the discoveries we have made God has allowed, and the answers we have found God has given us. He is noticeably in the minority among scientists.

To have faith in that which is not trustworthy leads to death, but many people do not even realize they are in peril. Their lives may be busy and in the world's eyes successful.

They may mistake busyness for joy. Yet, such a life is devoid of hope beyond this life, of purpose that does not pass away, and of the joy of knowing the Lord.

The Psalmist wrote, "For our heart rejoices in Him, because we trust in His holy name" (Ps. 33: 21). But how can we do that while we or those we know are suffering, or when the suffering of the world seems overwhelming? The Apostle Peter teaches us how to rejoice in the face of suffering by reminding us to stay focused on our great God, and the eternal life He has promised us in Jesus Christ. Peter writes:

> Blessed *be* the God and Father of our Lord Jesus Christ, who according to His abundant mercy has begotten us again to a living hope through the resurrection of Jesus Christ from the dead, to an inheritance incorruptible and undefiled and that does not fade away, reserved in heaven for you, who are kept by the power of God through faith for salvation ready to be revealed in the last time. In this you greatly rejoice, though now for a little while, if need be, you have been grieved by various trials, that the genuineness of your faith, *being* much more precious than gold that perishes, though it is tested by fire, may be found to praise, honor, and glory at the revelation of Jesus Christ, whom having not seen you love. Though now you do not see *Him*, yet believing, you rejoice with joy inexpressible and full of glory, receiving the end of your faith—the salvation of your souls (1 Pet. 1:3-9, NKJV).

Let's look more closely at what Peter is saying: (1) We are born again. (2) We have the hope of heaven because Jesus was resurrected. (3) Unlike our earth and our bodies, heaven is imperishable. (4) Our inheritance of heaven is kept safe by God's power through our faith. (5) Because of all that God has done for us, we have a reason to greatly rejoice.

And we can keep on rejoicing, Peter says, "though now for a little while, if need be, you have been grieved by various trials...." How long is a little while? We saw in the first chapter how important it is to remember that God's time is not our time. It's like the Family Circus cartoon in which Billy's teacher asks him how long a minute is. He asks back, "Is that a real minute, or a 'Wait a minute?'" Time is relative. The little while we suffer on earth is in contrast to the *eternity* God has waiting for us. To show us that contrast is one of the reasons God lets us suffer. The little while we suffer may be our whole life on earth. It is still but a moment compared to the glory waiting for us.

"If need be...." Some people to whom Peter was writing were being arrested, tortured, and killed for their faith. The Roman historian Suetonius tells us in his writings that Nero Caesar, emperor of Rome from A.D. 54-68, began to legally inflict persecution upon Christians even before he blamed them for the burning of Rome in A.D. 64 and ordered the persecution of Christians with a vengeance. For some, persecution was unavoidable. When God lets us suffer, however, it is His very power and grace that helps us hold onto our faith. And it is our faith and trust, and the presence of God's Spirit in our lives, which produces great joy.

Peter further notes that in suffering we may be "grieved by various trials." Grief is profound. It breaks the heart. I was grieved when my first husband left me for another woman. I was grieved when my second husband died. I am grieved that most of our family is unsaved and face eternity without God. I am grieved that Jesus had to die on the cross for my sins. You may be experiencing grief as you read these words. Still, because of all that God has done for us in Jesus, and because of the glories of heaven that await us, we can "greatly rejoice" in the midst of our grief.

Suffering can be a necessity to bring to the center of one's life the "genuineness of your faith." For some, suffering—especially the suffering of persecution—was a necessary test of faith. Peter points out that gold is a precious metal refined of impurities by fire. But we are far more precious to God than gold, and so the genuineness of our faith might be tested through suffering so that we "may be found" to give praise and honor and glory to God.

There's an old saying, "The proof is in the pudding." So it is with the faith of human beings. One can talk about faith at length and even brag about it. But until our faith is put into practice it isn't faith at all. Perhaps the most dramatic way we can show our trust in God is through our faith in suffering.

Peter's comments on the testing of one's faith is not unique to any particular people or generation. Three men who clung to their faith in God during the Babylonian captivity of the Jewish people (586-516 B.C.) were severely tested. In the third chapter of Daniel we read that King Nebuchadnezzar erected a huge golden statue 90 feet high. All citizens and captive peoples in Babylon were required to fall to their knees and worship the image—and all Babylonian gods—whenever music was played throughout the empire. But three Jews of great faith—Shadrach, Meshach and Abednego—refused to bow down to a worthless idol.

The penalty for refusing the king's edict was death in "a furnace of blazing fire." When Nebuchadnezzar discovered that the three men would worship only the one true God, he was so furious that he ordered the furnace to be heated seven times hotter than usual. It was so hot that the soldiers who led Shadrach, Meshach and Abednego to the furnace were killed by the intense heat.

But the three faithful Jews were not. King

Nebuchadnezzar was amazed to see not three but four men walking in the furnace. "Look! I see four men loosed and walking about in the midst of the fire without harm, and the appearance of the fourth is like a son of the gods!" (Dan. 3:25).

When the three men came out of the furnace it was discovered that the fire had not even singed their hair. The King was so astounded (who wouldn't be!) that he ordered worship of the Jewish God to be allowed in his kingdom. And he caused Shadrach, Meshach and Abednego to prosper in Babylon.

These three Jews proved their faith by willingly being thrown into the fire. God was with them. Nebuchadnezzar believed that God sent an angel to protect them. Some scholars believe it must have been the Son of God, Jesus Himself. One thing we can be certain of is that when God in his infinite wisdom allows us to suffer various trials, Jesus will be with us.

Peter wrote his first letter partly from his experiences of suffering. More than once he was thrown into prison for preaching that Jesus was the promised Messiah (Acts 5 and 12). Each time an "angel of the Lord" rescued him. No wonder the early Church was so filled with joy. Even in suffering—especially in suffering—they continually experienced God's grace and power.

And so Peter could write, "Though now you do not see Him, yet believing, you rejoice with joy inexpressible and full of glory." Joy never left the persecuted Church. Luke writes in Acts 13:52, "And the disciples were continually filled with joy and with the Holy Spirit." Even in sorrow and grief the joy of the Lord comforts us and causes us to bring praise and honor and glory to our Savior Jesus Christ. I cannot think of any greater calling than to bring praise and honor and glory to God.

Peter's words are the heart of faith. They are the keys to

the whole puzzle of how to suffer with joy. It is only through trusting God's promises, through faith that Christ died for our sins, that we can have eternal life, that we can be filled with "joy inexpressible and full of glory."

We began the book with God's promise in Romans 8:28, "And we know that God causes all things to work together for good to those who love God, to those who are called according to *His* purpose." "And we know" (we know that we know—that is our faith). "That God causes" (He is all-powerful; He interacts in our lives). "All things" (the good and bad, our sin and our pain and our joy). "To work together for good" (God knows what is good for us more than we do). "To those who love God" (love is a choice; we choose to love God with all our hearts, with all our souls, with all our strength and minds). "To those who are called according to His purpose" (God has a purpose for each of us).

My life is a testimony to the truth of this verse. Although I could not see His hand in my suffering when I was a child, I knew God was there. When my first husband grew cold and distant, God was my companion. My husband might leave us, but I knew that God wouldn't. At the custody hearing, when the lawyer asked the role of religion in my life, I replied that with God we could be joyful even when our hearts are broken. When my second husband's temper flare-ups did not diminish as our financial lives got better, God's Word provided comfort, strength, and the certainty that God disapproved of the outbursts. When my second husband died, God was there, holding me up each day.

I knew I belonged to God when I started keeping company with my sweetheart, a born again Christian. He not only led me to Christ, he has encouraged and supported me throughout this ministry. God did, indeed, cause all of the hurt in my life to work together for good, not only my good, but to His praise and glory. This book is part of His purpose for me.

Through His Word and His Spirit, God will give us the strength we need, not only to endure, but also to "greatly rejoice with joy inexpressible and full of glory" (1 Pet. 1:8), regardless of His reason for letting us suffer. Being reassured that He is in control, that He loves us and that He always has a reason is enough.

Index to Bible References

Old Testament

Genesis
2:15-17 35
3:12 37
3:13 37
15:13 91
35:18 132

Exodus
2:23-24 94
3:21-22 92
9:26 92
12:21-27 83
12:35-36 92
12:37-38 95
12:42 100
13:8 100
14:10-12 132
20:5 111
20:6 27
22:21 97
23:9 97

Leviticus
16 63
19:34 97
20:26 145

Numbers
6:2-21 39

Deuteronomy
5:10 27
6:5 132
10:12-13 41
10:19 97
27:14-26 135
28:2-14 135
28:9-10 122
28:15 50
28:15-68 135
32:43 87

Joshua
2 110
6:18-19 49
7:6-9 49
7:19-26 50
7:21 49

Judges
6:1 74
6:15 74
7:2 74
8:24-27 76
13:2-7 39

1 Samuel
8:7 87

2 Samuel
12:13-14 120
11-18 54

1 Kings
22:19 134

2 Chronicles
7:19-20 65

Job
1:1-3 123
1:4-5 123
1:6-8 124
1:13-19 124
1:20-21 125
1:21 137
1:22 125
2:9 125
2:10 125
24 22
38-40 22
42:10-17 128

Psalms
10 7
19:1-2 21
22:1-18 134
33:21 149
56:8 55
56:8-11 128
103:14 61
119:50 78
119:169 31
136 64

Proverbs
1:28-31 39
3:5 148
3:11-12 58
16:4 144
16:9 13
21:2 21
30:8-9 72

Ecclesiastes
3:1-8 8

Isaiah
1:18 25
5:21 131
6:1-3 134
53 134
53:6 98
53:7 86
55:8 . . . . .15, 20
61:1-3 134

Jeremiah
1:5 34

Daniel
3:25 152
12:2 133

Micah
5:2 134
6:8 81

New Testament

Matthew
3:17 98
5:11-12 122
5:14 130
5:44 24
6:14 24
6:19 82
6:19-21 138
8:19-20 98
11:28-29 99
12:50 35
17:5 98
17:24-27 129
22:37-40 61
23:13 54
25:46 133
26 86
26:42 .... 85, 143
26:69-75 98
27 86

Mark
6:11 87
12:30 132
13:11 126
14:34-36 85
14:36 85
14:50 84
14:66-72 84
15:34 84

Luke
1:37 94
9:23 79
12:22-24 135
12:29-31 135
16:19-31 133
19:38 83
21:14-15 126
22:42 85
22:43 85
22:44 85
23:34 .... 87, 127
23:39-43 127

23:41-42 88
23:43 88

John
3:16 147
7:5 84
8:24 134
8:34 137
9 110
9:2-3 111
9:30-33 113
11:4 114
11:21-22 115
11:25-26 115
11:32-33 115
11:35 115
11:45 116
12:9 116
13:33 84
13:34 84
14:2 138
14:6 27
14:15 .... 27, 41, 64
14:16 .... 64, 65
14:23-24 64
15:10 64
15:12-15 84
15:19 145
16:7-8 65
16:8 66

Acts
4:1-4 27
5 152
7:58 29
9:1-9 29
9:23-30 97
12 152
13:50 97
13:52 152
14:5-6 97
14:19 97
17:5-10 97

18:12-17 97
18:18 40
21:27 97
26:32 97
27:9-44 97

Romans
1:29 121
3:23 61
6:17-18 137
7:15 41
7:19 .... 41, 98
8:18 139
8:28 .. 2, 12, 16, 30, 34, 153
8:29 79
8:29-30 34
12:17-21 24
12:19 87
13:9-10 61

1 Corinthians
10:13 63
12:13-14 96

2 Corinthians
1:4 97
12:7-10 77
12:9 68

Galatians
5:22 122

Ephesians
1:4-5 34

Philippians
3:10 79
4:7 101

1 Thessalonians
4:17 11
5:9 134

Index to Bible References

2 Timothy
3:16 12
4:18 144

Titus
3:3-6 96

Hebrews
5:8 81
13:3 100

James
1:2 77
2 64

1 Peter
1:3 121
1:3-9 149
1:8 154
2:19-21 80
3:15 126
3:16-17 126
4:15-16 121

1 John
2:16-17 122
4:14 80

Revelation
3:19 66

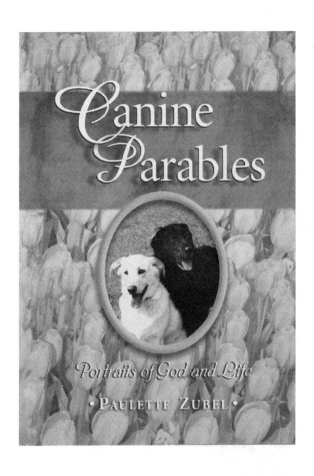

63 DEVOTIONALS TO REMIND US
THAT GOD IS OUR BEST FRIEND

Available at your favorite bookstore
or call **1-800-463-7818** • All major credit cards accepted
Magnus Press, P.O. Box 2666, Carlsbad, CA 92018

FREE Shipping & Handling on any size telephone order (U.S. orders only)

Great Books to Enrich Your Life!

What the Church Owes the Jew
~Leslie B. Flynn

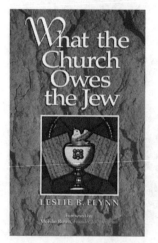

What do you know about the unique Jewish contribution to the Scriptures, the Church, and to the world at-large? Dr. Leslie Flynn, who served as pastor to many Jewish Christians in the New York area, passionately shares these answers and more (e.g., anti-Semitism, the Jewishness of Jesus), to help Jews and non-Jews build bridges of understanding and friendship.
ISBN 0-9654806-3-1 paper $12.00

Positive Attitudes for the 50+ Years:
How Anyone Can Make Them Happy & Fulfilling
~Willard A. Scofield

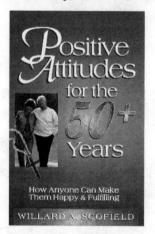

Looking for answers to some of the uncertainties of the 50+ Years? Willard Scofield, former associate editor for *Decision* magazine, and a Peale Center Guidance Counselor, shares insights to 75 often asked questions. Whether you have spiritual, financial, personal, relational, or other questions, you will find the answers in this helpful, biblically-based handbook.
ISBN 0-9654806-2-3 paper $12.00

Yes We Can Love One Another!
Catholics and Protestants Can Share A Common Faith
~Warren Angel

You've heard and read a lot about the things Catholics and Protestants don't have in common!
Here's a book which tells you what we *do* have in common. You don't have to change churches to learn how to love other believers in Jesus Christ. Warren Angel helps remove barriers to fellowship by breaking down misconceptions Christians believe about each other, and shows us how, in Christ, we can be a Church of power and joy in the Holy Spirit.
ISBN 0-9654806-0-7   paper $12.00

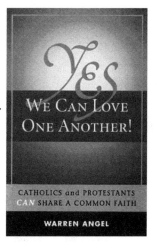

Jesus in the Image of God: *A Challenge to Christlikeness*
~Leslie B. Flynn

A great book for Bible study groups!
Here's a real antidote to the negative and faithless views of the Jesus Seminar. Let the Jesus of the Gospels challenge you to become more like him—the Son of God created in God's own image, who overcame despair, sorrow, rejection, and humiliation to bring healing, redemption, hope, and the Good News of God's love to all human beings.
ISBN 0-9654806-1-5   paper $12.00

Available at your favorite bookstore
or call **1-800-463-7818** • All major credit cards accepted
Magnus Press, P.O. Box 2666, Carlsbad, CA 92018
FREE Shipping & Handling on any size telephone order (U.S. orders only)